WORSHIP REVEALED

A THINKING WORSHIPER'S PRIMER

JEREMY PAPE

FIRST EDITION

Graphics and cover art created by Small Table Studio

Author headshot by Jesse Vadnais Photography

ISBN-13:

978-0692390924 (Small Table Studio)

ISBN-10:

0692390928

To Amber,
my favorite

CONTENTS

A PREEMPTIVE APOLOGY

CONCERNING THE SUBTITLE

The subtitle, "A Thinking Worshiper's Primer", is not an attempt to categorize or give license to prideful intellectualism. The subtitle is actually aimed to help fulfill a need among people that, frankly, need it. This is not to divide people into camps of worshipers that feel and worshipers that think. Everyone both thinks and feels. This is not about categorizing readers into warring tribes like some nightmare Myers Briggs personality test[1]. The reason I subtitled this book "A Thinking Worshiper's Primer" is to catch the attention of those who find themselves frustrated by the cacophony of brain-spraining "except when" and "only if" holes left in many of the conclusions offered concerning worship. Don't hear what I am not saying. I'm all about feelings, but we are more than feeling. We are more than thinking. We aspire to be fully whole people. So this is a not a primer for the unfeeling, but the thinking and feeling whole worshiper who may overlook this book without a specific call from something as arbitrary yet potentially divisive as a mere subtitle.

---

[1] "The Myers & Briggs Foundation." The Myers & Briggs Foundation. Web. 04 Nov. 2013.

INTRODUCTION

Hi. My name is Jeremy. I am a thinker. I am a worshiper. I am many things.

I am married to a smoking hot wife and have two amazing boys. I am sometimes petty and subject to flashes of unconcealable cynicism. I am opinionated, probably struggle with depression, and have an unhealthy relationship with caffeine. I also have a very organizational and strategic mind and can easily see the connections and relationships between the seemingly unrelated. I have a fondness for nice things, love the mountains, and am proudly introverted. I have done my fair share of worship leading on both the large and small scale. My public expressions of worship have mostly taken the form of liturgical and musical corporate experiences. My not-so-public journey of worship paints me to be very diversified. I have from time to time worshiped food, relationships, and even image. I have also worshiped the real and living God.

I'm complicated. I'm in process. We all are.

One of my favorite things is magic tricks. Whenever someone pulls out a deck of cards or saws someone in half I am sent back in time and become a child all over again. I know it's all an illusion, but I still love the "being tricked" part of a good magic trick. My wife is the opposite. She wants to figure it out. She wants to know about the trap door in the Pharaoh's Coffin. She wants to understand why the magician's assistant can only levitate while lying down in one particular outfit, but not when she is standing up and wearing pants. Not me. I love the mystery. I love the wonder.

I guess there are more people out there like my wife than like me because a few years ago I caught a glimpse of this show on television called "Magic's Biggest Secrets Revealed". The program starts like any typical magic show. A magician performs a trick with the help of his lovely assistant named something like Yvonne or Bambi. Soon all of us mere mortals are captivated by his bravery and skill as he defies death and suspends the laws of physics. But then the show takes a sharp turn toward the unconventional. The magician proceeds to brazenly break the first commandment of the magician's code. He proceeds to tell the television viewing audience how it's all done. He invites the cameras to come around to the back of the props as he points out the strings and mirrors. The magic trick is revealed to be just that, a trick, and the viewer is finally able to make sense of why the magician has been wearing a ski mask the whole time. It must be to keep his identity hidden from some magician militia or being blacklisted from whatever social events magicians have together. I don't know.

I usually turn the channel before the explanation because I don't want to know how they do it. I don't want an understanding of mirror management or wire theory to stifle the magician's spell over me or hinder his awe-inspiring trickery.

This is where magic and worship are very different. You might even say they are opposites. Whereas magic becomes lifeless and stale for us the more we understand or know about how it works, worship becomes more vibrant and breath taking. The sad thing is, too many of us treat worship the same way I treat magic, keeping out of the know to keep the magic alive. It's almost as if we are scared that if we look under the stage or peek behind the curtain of our favorite expressions of worship we will find it all to be a bunch of mirrors and strings set up to intensify misdirection and emotional sleight of hand. The truth is, we find the opposite. When we take the time for the longer, closer look at how God created us to worship, we find an amazing design that actually amplifies our worship potential instead of diminishing it. It is not to my or anyone's advantage to approach the topic of worship the same way I approach magic - staying stupid to protect the spectacle.

I will be the first to admit that there are plenty of mysteries concerning life, the world, and everything in it that are just impossible to solve this side of Heaven. However, there are some fundamental questions that must be explored and answered as we aspire to worship in both spirit and truth on this side of Eden. We all have our own personal, winding worship journey, but there are a few of worship's biggest secrets that need to be revealed for the good of us all. Some of the most foundational yet neglected worship mysteries do have both very understandable and extremely practical answers. Those answers and applications make up the content of this book. But before we can get to the right answers, we must take a step back to first ask the right questions.

Some Of Worship's Biggest Secrets

Any magician of notable skill understands much more than how to mindlessly repeat some seemingly arbitrary setup of strings and mirrors in hopes to replicate the same trick over and over again. They understand and even exploit some basic and foundational truths. For instance, one such truth is that in the right light, the unaided eye can't tell the difference between a clean mirror and an endless hallway. The magician's mastery of this and other realities concerning human perception precedes and dictates the placement of the very first mirror. This is arguably the difference between a great master of illusion and a two bit hack. If we apply the same argument to the topic of worship and worship leading, the next few questions are game changers.

What if we could understand how we are made to worship? I don't mean just in our spirits, but as whole people? We are made with not only a sensitivity to the supernatural, but also with senses and skin and bone and muscles and likes and dislikes. Does our physical interaction with the world play into our spiritual engagement with God and the worship of Him? If so, how?

Here's an obvious one. What exactly is worship? I'm not talking about some just off the top of your head definition either. What if you had to write it out with ink that would never fade and never be erasable for all eternity? And then what if you had to sign your name next to it? How do you define it in a way that is actually usable or helpful? How do you capture something seemingly so transcendent, so mysterious or wrapped in awe and wonder without your words ending up hollow?

More personally, the world is full of spiritual people. I am convinced that our conversation about worship has to start at a place so basic that it stands independent of any specific expression or object of worship. I am a follower of Jesus. So I also want to know what a Christ follower's pursuit of worship looks like. Why exactly is the topic of worship so important to being a disciple of Christ?

Being painfully practical, what if you're not feeling "it", whatever "it" is. What if you don't feel spiritual for a whole week? What if you don't feel connected for a whole month? What if you go a whole year and nothing seems able to divine the location of that "worshipy" feeling you experienced in the past?

Is there a way to consistently worship? Is there a way to get back to that place where you feel like every fiber of your being is pointing to and responding to the sheer greatness and goodness of God without being a giant hypocrite in the process?

These are some of the first questions we must ask to gain a basic understanding of both ourselves and worship if we want to get any real answers or useful understanding. Without knowing that the human eye cannot track the speed of the hand, all the magicians in the world talking about how to tie strings and place mirrors amounts to nothing more than hunches and trial and error guess work. Without understanding how our God-given form follows our God-given function to worship, we are grasping at straws. These relationships must be addressed and understood before any seemingly more practical or pressing conversation about method or mode can be fruitful.

As long as we treat these and other key questions like undecipherable magic tricks, we will continue to be contented with the occasional worshiper's "high" and live lives far less inspired and vibrant than God made us to live. We must take the magic trick out of our understanding of worship. We can no longer complacently settle for the occasional happy worship accident. I'm inviting you to bring your questions, concerns, and your best critical thinking to an all-access backstage tour of worship. So turn your thinking caps to eleven, get some caffeine, and follow me behind the curtain, past the lights, to get up close and personal with worship. It's time for worship to be truly revealed.

About this Book

"You'll have things you want to talk about. I will too."

Growing up, I daily heard these words sung by Mister Rogers at the end of every television broadcast of Mr. Roger's Neighborhood. It acknowledged that there is always more to talk about. The same is true for this book. After reading it, I fully expect you to have some things you want to talk about. This book won't get into many of the topics typically addressed by publications concerning the practice or facilitation of corporate worship. We won't get into auditions, crafting music, team dynamics, excellence and authenticity, or even what makes a meaningful, repeatable practice different from a tired ritual. These and other nuts-and-bolts topics have been exhaustively covered by more culturally narrow or era specific publications. Also, this book is not going to sell you the "cool" you need for your ministry to grow. It will not give you ten steps to becoming the greatest worship leader ever or even how to be better than the worship leader at the church across the street. This book aims to take one giant step back from those topics under the umbrella of worship and take a long fresh look at the worship umbrella itself. Consequently, the giant step back offered in the following pages will greatly clarify and give perspective to any future conversations addressing the aforementioned omissions.

This book is super-duper linear. There's a part of me that wants to have the cool disclaimer of more lateral works admonishing you to skip around or even to the end. However, if you work through the content in your own way and leisure, it will only lead to more confusion. Without the careful, systematic formation of a theological and logical baseline understanding of worship itself, we will soon find ourselves rehashing some of the same symptomatic, circular questions that have plagued those of us for which worship is still mostly a magic trick. Of course, my end goal is not to be linear, but to clearly offer a place of common ground to make the intergenerational worship conversation accessible to any and every-one. For our understanding of worship to be foundational enough to support our own beliefs, it must be able to support all beliefs. To come to any useful conclusions about any manifestations of worship in our present day, our conclusions must be transcendent of all eras. We must find the starting line for all of humanity first and let rest of the conversation follow.

Additionally, often books with the word "worship" in the title are written primarily for worship leaders with a cursory invitation for all the regular folks to listen in and maybe learn something. Let me be clear. This book is for everyone. This is especially the case since all worship leaders are, after all, intrinsically worshipers as well. We are all worshipers. You, reading this book on your Kindle on the train from work, are a worshiper. Me, like every other book writing tool in Starbucks, am a worshiper. The kid smoking a joint while she checks her stocks on her iPhone is a worshiper. So I have included a brief note to worshipers and a letter to worship leaders at the end of every chapter followed by some additional questions for reflection. These offer a little space to either quickly expand on the chapter's contents in a more specific, audience-focused nature or touch on something that didn't quite fit into the larger work that I believed to be edifying for most. They are the extra features of this book much like the extra features you might find on a DVD or Blu-Ray. I highly encourage you to read them all, but feel free to skip them if you are reading this book for homework or having a reading race.

Note To Worshipers #1

Hello fellow worshiper,

You know, the beginning of anyone's journey to becoming a follower of Christ includes a moment when they are overwhelmed with the truth of God's goodness and greatness. This first response could be described as many things, but it is definitely in part a response of worship. Truth be told, when all the cards are played, lots of things will come to an end when Christ returns but worship will continue for all eternity. I think this makes a pretty good case for why it is worth our time to be good students of worship. Who wants to spend the rest of their Earthly lives with only vague feelings about worship and its part in our relationship to the real God of the Bible?

Not this guy.

But so often great worship experiences seem more like a happy accident. They can seem to lack any rhyme or reason. I'm here to tell you that worship does not have to be that way for us or anyone. It just takes a little time and study to gain some clarity and even start to make your own contribution to the larger worship conversation.

Oh yeah. Don't let my common use of corporate expressions of worship throw you off the scent of the deeper, central worship principles in this book. I figure that the large group worship experience is the one most commonly and frequently experienced by most followers of Christ. I use it only as a context to help explain and introduce deeper, fundamental truths that transcend any specific expression or even object of worship. They are not my attempt to get some op-ed word in. They are simply a common example.

Mostly, I'm just honored that you are joining me in the conversation. Worship, if anything, is an expression of love. We are clearly commanded to "Love the Lord your God with all your heart and with all your soul and with all your mind and with all your strength." (Emphasis mine)[2] If this book or the ideas in it get overwhelming, take a second to remember that our effort to worship God with all our mind is in itself an act of worship.

Sincerely,

Jeremy

---

[2] "Mark 12:13." The Holy Bible: New International Version. Grand Rapids, MI: Zondervan, 2005. Print.

Letter To Worship Leaders - i

Dear worship leader, lead worshiper, or whatever you like to be called,

A few years ago I was turned onto the book "Into Thin Air: A Personal Account of the Mt. Everest Disaster" by Jon Krakauer[3]. It's this epic story about people trying to summit the tallest mountain on the planet. Specifically one attempt in the late 90's that cost eight climbers their lives. Before reading this book I was vaguely in the know concerning how one approaches the climbing of Mount Everest. I knew there were base camps and Sherpas and stuff. I knew that summiting Everest probably wasn't something you did on a weekend whim akin to deciding to go into the city. But after reading this book, a whole new dimension of preparation, not only for the climbers mentioned in this specific account, but anyone making an attempt for the summit was revealed. You have to train for as much as years. You have to get passports. You have to get serious permission. You have to hike for miles to even get to what I used to think was the starting line, base camp. It's as if the preparation to even set foot on the mountain is a test for the mental toughness and physical endurance it will take to successfully summit Everest. Before reading this book I had always assumed you could just helicopter in, pick a Sherpa, and get your climb on. But now a whole world of necessary but previously unknown info and prep has been revealed to me. The climb starts way before any arrival at base camp.

So what does this have to do with worship? The conversation concerning worship in this generation has lived almost entirely at the base-camp level. All our worship conversations in one form or another have centered around things like "the five essential techniques" or "ten best practices"

---

[3] Krakauer, Jon. Into Thin Air: A Personal Account of the Mount Everest Disaster. New York: Villard, 1997. Print.

that should be in every worship leader's backpack. Regardless of our intentions or platitudes, the worship conversation has grown from and formed around the assumption that the act or manifestation of our worship is the hub of the conversation. This is just like my wrong assumptions concerning where and when an Everest summit attempt starts. It is short-sighted and naive to start our worship conversation already at the metaphorical base camp stage. Doing so often creates patterns of misunderstanding and slavery. It can lead to broken relationships with each other and sometimes God. Instead we must start our worship conversation at the metaphorical preparation stage before one even gets to Nepal. Don't get me wrong. It would be hard to overstate the importance of our worship acts or the working role of base camp on Mount Everest. However, it is disastrous if either are wrongly perceived as the ultimate starting line.

My hope is that this book might have a similar effect on our understanding of worship as "Into Thin Air" had on my understanding of climbing Mount Everest. I want to take a giant step back to gain a new perspective on the worship conversation. I want to restart at the actual starting line, the preparation. I don't mean our preparation, but the preparation of God. If He designed us to do anything, it is to worship. That is the true start of any foundational understanding of worship for our generation and the next generation, and the starting line of this book.

Thank you for joining the conversation. God be with us all.

Sincerely,

Jeremy Pape

Introduction Discussion Questions

Describe a powerful worship experience in your own life.

What questions would you love to have answered concerning worship?

What do you think about the premise that everyone is a worshiper?

ONE

HARDWIRED TO PERCEIVE

Growing up, I loved to look at cross-section diagrams of just about any-thing. I would pore over page after oversized page of library books detail-ing castles with moats, high towers, and brutal arsenals of medieval war-fare defense mechanisms. The subject matter has grown with me; Star Wars spaceships on to fighter jets and then house plans, but the fun of seeing the way parts of a whole work together and complement each other to form a functional design has always mesmerized me.[4] I'm amazed that someone out there can draw these intricate illustrations and has the knowledge and understanding of the subject matter to draw it accurately. I'm not a terrible artist but if I tried to draw a basic gas engine to scale with all the parts of a transmission, exhaust, and fuel system, let's just say you wouldn't want my drawings to be part of your starting pitch to a major car manufacturer. My drawings would be embarrassing guess work at best and probably get you laughed out of the room.

---

[4] Star Wars. Twentieth-Century Fox Corp., 1977.
Yeah, you might want to join the rest of the century and give this a viewing if you haven't already.

I mean, what's a manifold and where does it even go?

But you know who could draw a scale cross section of a gas motor without any outside help? I bet we've all met mechanics who could, no problem, and the manifold would be perfectly placed. Any first year car designer could draw it in their sleep. Not all of them could just sit down and diagram every Ferrari or every Mustang model, maybe someone can, but they ALL could draw a basic gas motor to scale. This is not because they passed the "How to draw a basic gas motor" class in college, but because they are so intimately familiar with all the components and working parts that make a gas motor work. They can "build" the motor on the paper as they draw it. They know how the different parts work together to such a degree that the drawing practically draws itself.

Obviously, I am no car designer. I am absolutely fine with taking my car to Jiffy Lube and paying them to change my oil.[5] I don't need to know how a gas engine works. I just need to know where to pull up my car so that nice people in blue shirts can work their automotive magic.

Now, before some of you gear-heads and oil-monkeys throw this book across the room and demand the resignation of my "man card" for having someone else change my oil, let me make my point. My point is, if you're still reading, that any follower of Christ, not the casual dabbler in spirituality or the religious event attender, but those who call themselves worshipers of the most high God, must similarly understand some basic working parts of worship or they may, themselves, entirely miss out on what it is to worship. It is NOT okay for us to pull our lives up to some spiritual hub and let someone else work their "worship magic" on us so that we feel better about the world, God, and ourselves. Unlike an oil

---

[5] "Oil Change Service I Car Maintenance Service - Jiffy Lube." Oil Change Service I Car Maintenance Service - Jiffy Lube. Web. 04 Nov. 2013.

change, no one can worship for you. We have to wrap our minds around the basic workings of worship or be ready to turn in our "worshiper" card. That goes double, if not triple, for self-professed worship leaders. We don't all need to be able to diagram the complete workings of every worship practice or expression. We do need to be able to mentally diagram a basic understanding of key moving parts and how they move together.

In the pursuit of clarity, let me give you another analogy. When my young son sees a moving car, he assumes the car goes because the wheels are rolling. However, when he gets older, he'll hear about engines or come face to face with his first breakdown. He will quickly come to understand that all the real action happens under the hood. Sure, it's the wheels that turn, but a motor is turning those wheels and if the motor quits, the wheels stop and the car fails to go. In the same way, some might assume that when I propose that worship has moving parts, that I am getting ready to talk about style or drums or stage lighting or music. As valid and important as those conversations can be, they are topics more on the level of wheel brand or paint color rather than the engine. Just as our understanding of cars has grown with us, worship at first glance can seem to be working because of outward factors, but as we mature, we come to understand that all the real action is happening under the hood, inside us. So let's take our first step toward a mature understanding of worship and turn our attention inward, to the inner workings of ourselves, to where all the real action is. Let's take a look under the hood.

No On Or Off Switch

The first look under the hood reveals the truth that we are all hardwired to perceive. Let me explain. I love walking in the mountains. It feels like the higher I get, the closer I am to God. I love the smell of the pine trees, the shuffle crunch of the path beneath my feet, and the taste of perfectly clean air. I love the cold patches of snow in stark defiance of the warm, naked sun and the mountains; remaining resolute to reach, stretch, and touch just one of the quilted stars even if it takes another millennium to do so. Now, before I start my hike, I don't have to concentrate on starting up my eyes and ears and feet. I don't have a tasting switch or a button that turns my ability to smell off and on. (I have changed enough diapers to have thoroughly looked for one. If I had such a button, I would have found it by now.) No, I perceive the world around me automatically. I can't help it. It's hardwired into my being. We are all hardwired this way, to automatically perceive the world in both the extraordinary and the seemingly ordinary moments of our lives.

Extraordinary moments seem to suddenly appear or surprise us. All of us, at some time or another, have discovered or accidentally walked in on a sacred space or a holy moment. When we do, we know it just like Moses did when he found the burning bush.[6] He automatically perceived (both visually through the burning bush and audibly by hearing the statement "the place you stand is holy") and clued in on the fact that he had stumbled upon the extraordinary. I've never come across a burning bush, but I would describe some of my times in the mountains as holy. Maybe you're not a mountains nut like me, but there are vast oceans. Perhaps you're a star gazer purist; driving to exclusive vistas of night skies untamed by civilized lights. Maybe it's when you hold a baby or go running on a clear day. You might be an on-the-porch storm watcher. We are all born into a vast world of sensory stimulation. We all have favorites and we all perceive them automatically.

But what about the more ordinary moments of life? The day to day? Again, we don't just turn on our ability to perceive the world around us

---

[6] "Exodus 3:2." The Holy Bible: New International Version. Grand Rapids, MI: Zondervan, 2005. Print.

when we think a "good part" is coming. And that's a good thing. Even in that which we often take for granted or dismiss as commonplace, is part of an entire world bursting with sensory detail. Take for instance something as common as the four seasons. Each season is common only in its inevitable changing. Truly, the seasons are a functional extravagance in which sights, sounds, smells and tastes, incapable of co-existence, seamlessly dance in and out of our world so that we might experience and enjoy them all. In a world of only spring, we would welcome the explosion of green and wild flowers but entirely miss out on the golden, orange forests of fall. While hot chocolate is thick and creamy in the winter, in the summer, it's a gooey, heavy-in-your-guts mess. Even the most ordinary, drawn out, seemingly endless moments of existence are long because we are incapable of not perceiving every stimuli packed second.

The automatic and unchanging perceptive wiring in us secures our front row seat to creation, whether we pay attention or not. "Extraordinary" and "ordinary" are merely points of view to be captivated by or bored with, but our perception of the world around us is constant, untiring, and intrinsically built in. Understanding how we are hardwired to perceive is our first step on the journey of revealing worship.

Our next steps are guided by a couple of questions. God was the one who designed us to perceive automatically and all the time. So, what exactly are we supposed to perceive? How much does it matter if we perceive it or not? And by what means and to what end are we supposed to perceive whatever it is we are made to perceive? These questions lead us another step closer to a working understanding of worship. Let's start with the first one. What exactly are we hardwired to perceive anyway?

To Perceive What?

In the truly extraordinary moments, mountaintop experiences, snapshots of my life flooded by beauty and holy sensory overload, I find myself singing along with songwriter Sara Groves, "what if this was made for me?"[7] Not in a self-centered "It's all about me" kind of way, but more of a, "I'm reluctantly coming to terms with, and may be on the cusp of accepting, a scandalous truth" kind of way. It's like God, knowing I would find myself in this very place at this exact moment in history, filled this speck of the universe with sights, sounds, smells, tastes, and even textures suited especially perfect for me. And I drink it in. But for what end. What exactly are we drinking in? What exactly is it that God hardwired us to perceive? We find our answer in Psalm 19:1-6.

"1 The heavens declare the glory of God;

the skies proclaim the work of his hands.

2 Day after day they pour forth speech;

night after night they reveal knowledge.

3 They have no speech, they use no words;

no sound is heard from them.

4 Yet their voice goes out into all the earth,

their words to the ends of the world.

In the heavens God has pitched a tent for the sun.

5 It is like a bridegroom coming out of his chamber,

like a champion rejoicing to run his course.

6 It rises at one end of the heavens

and makes its circuit to the other;

nothing is deprived of its warmth."

It's God's glory. We are hardwired to perceive God's glory. Romans 1:20 confirms that God's glory is everywhere and accessible by everyone.

---

[7] Sara Groves. "Maybe There's A Loving God." All Right Here. Integrity Media, 2002. CD.

"For since the creation of the world God's invisible qualities—his eternal power and divine nature—have been clearly seen, being understood from what has been made, so that men are without excuse."

Creation is clearly dripping with His eternal power (His greatness) and His divine nature (His goodness). Isaiah 6:3 describes angels in heaven "calling to one another 'Holy, holy, holy is the LORD Almighty; the whole earth is full of his glory.'" It is to this end - that we would see His glory all around us - that He filled creation with his glory and hardwired us to first perceive it.

So if this is the reason we are able to sense the world around us, how important is it to God that we perceive his glory? I know God always has a reason for what he does, but where does perceiving His glory fall on the cosmic priority list?

A key indicator of how much something means to us is to what lengths we go to make it happen. If something is no big deal, we put it on the back burner. If it's important, we go the distance. But if it's our passion, if our desired results are paramount, we go above and beyond, obsess over every minute detail, and walk a thin line between laser-focused and fanatical to make sure it happens. It is by the extent of the means used to achieve an end, that we are able to derive the end's priority. The driving focus and motivating power with which this end (that we perceive God's glory) grips the heart of God, is best understood in the context of the degree in which God designed us with the means to do that very thing. Be forewarned. To understand the extent of how God enabled us to perceive His glory, and in turn understand its importance to God that we do, we must get our hands dirty with a little science.

Glory Receptors

We are all born with a key component crucial for worship of any kind to happen. It is not our voice or our hands or knees. Even without a working voice, fingers, or toes, you would have this particular piece of worship hardware in spades. Truthfully, it is more a collection of tiny parts that make up a whole than any one thing, and we are filled to the gills with them. Others call them nerve endings. I call them "glory receptors" and here's why. They are meticulously designed, crafted and supported by entire systems of muscle, sinew, and bone to optimize our ability to perceive as much of God's glory as possible. We can, and do, in fact, sense God. Not only in the cultural euphemism, "God showed up" (erroneously implying that the space you were in was previously devoid of God but later became occupied by Him), but in quite literal ways. Experiencing, identifying, and understanding God's glory through our senses is common fare throughout the Bible. Once you start to see it, you can't miss it. Let me walk through some examples of all our senses to illustrate at what prominence God holds the function of us perceiving His glory via the form of our glory receptors.

See

Think about your favorite places. If you're like me, scenery has huge weight in determining your favorites. It is amazing how Hi-def our view of the world is.

- Your eyes are composed of more than 2 million working parts.
- Both of your retinas contain 120 million rods for black, gray, and white, and 8 million cones that are color sensitive.
- Your eyes can process 36,000 bits of information every hour.
- Your eye is the only part of the human body that can function at 100% ability at any moment, day or night, without rest.
- Under the right conditions, your eye can see the light of a candle at a distance of 14 miles.[8]

---

[8] "101 Amazing Eye Facts." Lenstore. Web. 04 Nov. 2013.

Isaiah 40:26 instructs, "Lift up your eyes and look to the heavens. Who created all these? He who brings out the starry host one by one and calls forth each of them by name. Because of his great power and mighty strength, not one of them is missing." Psalm 96:6 tells us "The heavens proclaim his righteousness, and all the peoples see his glory."

In 1990, NASA launched the Hubble Telescope into orbit, giving us images of space never before seen in human history.[9] God made stars, planets and nebula, even entire galaxies, that he knew Adam, Abraham, and Moses would never see with their human eyes, but we would. Let that sink in. The images captured by the Hubble Telescope are of a scale, distance, and beauty only describable as awesome. Add to that sun-kissed mountain meadows, crystal water reefs, and snow covered pine forests, and it quickly becomes clear God made the visible world not only to be navigable by our eyes, but to unapologetically show off to our glory receptors.

Smell

For me, smell is the forgotten sense, that is, until it is needed. In this season of life, my wife and I are raising two little boys. I remember my nose being useful for many things. But for now, "stink detector" is its highest function. Here's how our little bundles of joy from God can stink so bad.

- Your nose contains 5 million olfactory neurons, plus their support cells and stem cells each topped by at least 10 hair-like cilia.
- It is estimated that each cilia cell has between 500 and 1,000 receptor proteins that are genetic in nature, and determine which odors our brains can detect and identify, according to which receptors are activated by the odor.

---

[9] "National Aeronautics and Space Administration." Main Hubble Page. Web. 04 Nov. 2013.

- Your nose can recognize up to 10,000 separate odors (supposing you aren't wracked with allergies).[10]

God reveals His love for the smell of fresh bread in Leviticus 2:9 as His instruction for the priest states, "He shall take out the memorial portion from the grain offering and burn it on the altar as an offering made by fire, an aroma pleasing to the LORD." We see God also was deeply moved by the smell of Bar-B-Q in Genesis 8:20-21 when "Noah built an altar to the LORD and, taking some of all the clean animals and clean birds, he sacrificed burnt offerings on it. The LORD smelled the pleasing aroma and said in his heart: 'Never again will I curse the ground because of humans, even though every inclination of the human heart is evil from childhood. And never again will I destroy all living creatures, as I have done.'" Good move Noah! I mean, who can stay angry when good food is on the grill? One of my favorite smells is ozone right after a good rain. I'm sure you have favorites too. God plugged us full of glory receptors to smell them all.

Taste

I can eat anywhere, anytime. I'll eat in front of the TV, while driving, or even when I'm bored with nothing better to do. (I know, don't try to count all the red flags concerning diet and nutrition I've just confessed). Eating can kind of be a "filler" activity for me. But when I taste something amazing, when I am surprised by flavory goodness, all I am gets laser-focused on the eating task at hand and everything else just fades into obscurity. I'm rendered virtually incorrigible to any end other than the immediate moment's savoring of deliciousness. Just look at how we are equipped to taste!

---

[10] "Learning About the Function of Our Sense of Smell." Learning About the Function of Our Sense of Smell. Web. 04 Nov. 2013.

- You have on average 9,000 taste buds.
- You have taste buds on your tongue, the roof of your mouth, pharynx and esophagus.
- Each taste bud contains over 100 cells and all buds react to the basic tastes.
- Our sense of taste is affected by all other senses (especially smell but also the sound of the "crunch", the food's color and even the feeling of burning or cooling caused by chilies or mint).[11]

Psalm 34:8 tells us to "Taste and see that the LORD is good; blessed is the man who takes refuge in him." And from that taste, 1 Peter 2:2-3 tells us "Like newborn babies, crave pure spiritual milk, so that by it you may grow up in your salvation, now that you have tasted that the Lord is good". Eating great-tasting food is part of who God made us to be. We are made, if anything, to connect our experiences and memories of great food to God's glory. You can't savor food that is imaginary or far away. God's glory is so real, so close, that you can taste it.

Touch

One of my love languages is touch. It doesn't have to be a big deal. A little pat on the back or a brush of my arm is all I sometimes need from my wife. Our sense of touch is so powerful, a little goes a long way.

- You have around 4 million nerve endings all over your skin.
- You have around 17,000 tactile receptors in your hand.[12]
- You have around 1,300 nerve endings per square inch in your hand.

---

[11] "8 Amazing Facts about Taste." 8 Amazing Facts about Taste. Web. 04 Nov. 2013.

[12] "Dermatology/little Help?" Dermatology: Little Help?, Free Nerve Endings, Tactile Receptors. Web. 04 Nov. 2013.

- Your palm can detect the presence of a weight only weighing a fraction of a gram.[13]

I can feel the warmth of being carried as I think about this description of God in Isaiah 40:11. "He tends his flock like a shepherd: He gathers the lambs in his arms and carries them close to his heart; he gently leads those that have young." We're not ensnared by an icy grip and jostled into place, but instead, gently held close and led. Warmth shifts to burning when Psalm 11:6 says "On the wicked he will rain fiery coals and burning sulfur; a scorching wind will be their lot." Both statements are very real because of the intricate detail and micro-engineering God used to build the sense of touch in all of us.

Hear

As a musician, when hypothetically asked to choose between sight and hearing, I always choose hearing. I'm way past looking at my hands and I've always been below poor at sight-reading. Ears are powerful tools in our perception of the world.

- Your ear can perceive frequencies from very, very deep bass around 20 cycles per second to really high pitch sounds at 20,000 cycles per second.
- In some frequency ranges, your ear can detect pitch changes as small as 3 tenths of one percent of the original frequency.[14]

Our ability to perceive the subtle differences as well as the expanse of sound is no accident. In 1 Kings 19:12 we lean in to hear that "After the earthquake came a fire, but the LORD was not in the fire. And after the fire came a gentle whisper." Our hair stands at attention at the unhar-

---

[13] "How Does the Sense of Touch Work?" WiseGEEK. Web. 04 Nov. 2013.

[14] "The Scientist and Engineer's Guide To Digital Signal Processing By Steven W. Smith, Ph.D." Human Hearing. Web. 04 Nov. 2013.

nessed power of this description found in 2 Samuel 22:14. "The LORD thundered from heaven; the voice of the Most High resounded." Sound gives all the other senses credibility. Lightning without thunder is a fun flash in the night, ocean waves simply end at the shoreline and the Death Star explosion is a fourth of July tennis ball on a wire.[15] But with sound, they boom-rattle the Earth, scream to a crash, and KA-DOOOOOOOOOM into oblivion. (That's 2 Star Wars references so far for those of you keeping track).

Spirit

I don't know if there are invisible "Holy Spirit ears" in our hearts or if all the other physical glory receptors have twin spiritual glory receptors, but regardless, we all can perceive the Holy Spirit. Sure there are very perceptible physical world effects of the Holy Spirit at work, but I'm talking about us actually sensing beyond the physical limits of our nerve endings. God has made in us a very specialized and real ability to sense supernatural stimuli. Luke 4:1 gives us a picture of the Holy Spirit filling and directing Jesus. It states, "Jesus, full of the Holy Spirit, left the Jordan and was led by the Spirit into the wilderness." Jesus was able to perceive and follow the Holy Spirit's direction. Another instance of the Holy Spirit allowing the supernatural being perceived is in Acts 7:55 when "Stephen, full of the Holy Spirit, looked up to heaven and saw the glory of God, and Jesus standing at the right hand of God." Even if we can't analyze and chart it in the same ways we can document and diagram the finely tuned workings of all our other senses, the fact remains that this sixth sense is built into all of us and it functions for the same reason as the others; that we would perceive copious amounts of God's glory.

---

[15] Star Wars. Twentieth-Century Fox Corp., 1977.

When I think of the vast array of glory receptors hardwired into each one of us, millions of nerve endings grouped and aligned to form our senses, it makes me think of acres of satellite dishes, each tuned in to receive a specific kind of signal. I imagine fields of solar panels that follow the Sun from end to end of the sky. God covered us inside and out with glory receptors that are constantly receiving stimuli from God. And of course, our glory receptors "cross train" in that they help us read visual body language cues, hear "that tone" from our mother, and even protect us from the danger of hot surfaces. But earlier, I described passion as going above and beyond, obsessing over detail and walking the thin line between laser focused and fanatical. When it comes to us being able to perceive His glory, God has uninhibitedly jumped over the line into categorical fanaticism. God went to unfathomable lengths to give us the ability to perceive His glory. It is of utmost importance to Him.

Don't Miss It

In a very true way, all of creation is for me and you, all of us really. But our crazy ability to perceive it is primarily a means to a very God-centered end. It is crystal clear that we are made to sense God's glory. And this is not an aside or learned function, this is hardwired into us so that "no man has an excuse". Our sensory hardwiring is extensive (even including a sixth sense that defies all wavelengths and pheromones) and we live in a world flooded with stimuli, pushing our highest thresholds of perception so that we might be wholesale overwhelmed by God's glory.

Sadly, we find ourselves easily missing it. If it's not a healing miracle or written on a wall, God's glory can be wrongly overlooked and tragically unnoticed. Why must it take huge, extravagant gifts like mountain ranges, ocean sunsets, or even healthy newborns for God's glory to get our attention? Did God dupe us by filling the earth with His glory only to design us to be limited and limping in our ability to perceive it? To quote the New Testament writer Paul, "By no means!"[16] Everything we have talked about thus far proves this is obviously not the case. We are plagued by an unfathomable number of glory receptors with no way to turn even one of them off.

No, God definitely did not trick us. But, perhaps we have been tricked. We have lost our wonder not only in the everyday little, but also in the special occasion big. So how do we get our sense of wonder back? We are well on our way to forming a foundation on which we can find some answers to that and other questions. But we must first peer a little longer under the hood at our own inner worship motors. It would be one thing if we were all like high-end cameras, perfectly designed to perceive God's glory and nothing more. But we are not cameras. There is another working part of our motor. It sits in the center of our countless glory receptors. It sets us apart from all other creation. We are not only hardwired to perceive, but we are rigged to respond.

---

[16] "Romans 6:2." The Holy Bible: New International Version. Grand Rapids, MI: Zondervan, 2005. Print.

A Note To Worshipers #2
concerning glory albums

Hey fellow worshiper,

Thank you so much for giving me some of your time to share my thoughts on worship. I am truly honored and humbled by it. I know this start to our conversation about worship might feel a little slow or impersonal or even too "sciencey" for you. That's okay. I know its relevant application may at first seem elusive, but we are well on our way in setting a life-long, lasting foundation of worship. For now, you can start to build what I call glory albums. Think of a family picture album, but instead of vacation pictures, it is full of memories of God's glory. This is an easy thing that can take any variety of forms, from journaling to an actual memory box filled with preserved keepsakes of creation. These glory albums can play a helpful role in fulfilling your desire to be a wholehearted worshiper of God. And it doesn't take much, just the occasional jotting down of an answered prayer or a picture of nature that left you breathless can make a great entry. Easy things you are already very capable of doing. I know life is always changing, and with it, our discretionary time, but if you just made one entry or gathered a single tangible memory every week, or even every month, you would quickly acquire a great collection. It is a small practice, but it will pay off in huge ways for you, just as it has for countless others, in your worship of God.

Again thanks for your time. As I write this, I'm excited and asking God to use this small book in a big way to bless and empower your worship of our awesome and glorious God.

Jeremy

A Letter To Worship Leaders - ii
concerning being tour guides

Dear worship tour guide,

God has already set the ball rolling by hardwiring the people you lead with enough glory receptors to make the Hubble Telescope look like a junior astronomy kit and, furthermore, their receptors are never off or down for maintenance. You don't have to replicate God's glory for people, but only point out the glory that's already flooding their senses. This reality gives you a solid starting line in planning strategies to facilitate your community worship of the living God. We all long to join God in His holy fanaticism, that people would see His glory. So a first step is to become skillful tour guides, pointing out God's glory as we journey with the people we lead. Incorporating a simple, concrete reminder of who God is or what he has done can literally be all the difference. God has already gifted you with the skills to set the table, you just have to let His glory be the main course.

I know we all have traditions, leadership cultures, or even pain-in-the-neck-congregants that may not be the most "conducive" in your pursuit to lead in this direction, but be assured, the changes don't have to be big to have a big impact. Little things like icebreaker questions about where people have seen God or simply connecting God to the day's beautiful weather can become second nature and maybe even begin to form new traditions in your community. Generations of worshipers and worship leaders have blessed following generations by first being great tour guides for God's glory.

Blessings to you and those God has trusted you to lead.

Humbly,

Jeremy Pape

Chapter 1 Discussion Questions

Tell about a time your senses where seemingly overloaded or completely filled.

What is your favorite sense?

Do you have a specific story or memory where you strongly experienced God's goodness and/or greatness?

TWO

RIGGED TO RESPOND

It's probably no surprise to you after two Star Wars references in the first chapter that I love science fiction. I like it all. Everything from short stories by Isaac Asimov and Orson Scott Card to summer blockbusters on the big screen. My brother introduced me to a particular medium that has always held a special place in my heart, the comic book. I love reading about extraordinary people overcoming insurmountable obstacles and saving the day at just the moment when all seems lost. In particular, I like comics about superheroes like Spider-Man, Batman, and Superman.[17] Who hasn't fantasized about being able to effortlessly climb up and down sheer walls? Solving crimes with beyond state of the art technologies in my underground crime lab and then saving the world with an arsenal of gadgets sounds like a day well spent to me. What can I say? I love the flying dream. All superheroes in the comics have amazing attributes that seem to place them above the rest of us "mere mortals". That is until you remember that we "mere mortals" are covered

---

[17] "Spider-Man" - Lee, Stan and Steve Ditko. Amazing Fantasy #15. Marvel Comics. 1962
"Batman" - Kane, Bob and Bill Finger. Detective Comics #27. DC Comics. 1939
"Superman" - Siegel, Jerry and Joe Shuster. Action Comics #1. DC Comics. 1939

head to toe in glory receptors that are hardwired to perceive vast amounts of stimuli 24/7/365. So what if Spider-Man has "spider sense". I can sense the Spirit of the living God. But as amazingly super as our ability to sense the world around us is, our ability to process, categorize and store that information really starts to look like science fiction. Except that it's not. It's how God made us. For those of you feeling less than super today, let me reintroduce you to a part of your worship engine that is anything but commonplace or "mere" anything.

Our Super Brain

So if our glory receptors (our senses) are automatically on all the time and if we are hardwired to perceive the stimuli constantly flooding our senses, what happens to all those bits of data? Are we just biological cameras that capture our senses? Does it all just go in one ear and out the other? Yes, if you're thirteen. But seriously, after our senses actually sense something, what happens next? The answer to this question can be found deeper inside our inner worship motors. This piece of hardware completes the perceiving function we are hardwired to do and sets us apart from all other creation. It weighs only 3 pounds and is roughly the size of a grapefruit but it is one of the most powerful and advanced processors known to man. It is the human brain, and understanding some basic concepts of its amazing design helps fill in some of the gaps in our understanding of worship. So don't wash your hands yet. There's a little more science to get our hands dirty with.

When stimuli comes in contact with our senses, it is shot to our super processor (our brain) were it is processed and stored via neurons. An adult brain has around 100 billion neurons.[18] That means that even the most average of us are capable of holding around 2.5 petabytes (or a mil-

---

[18] "What Is the Memory Capacity of the Human Brain?: Scientific American." What Is the Memory Capacity of the Human Brain?: Scientific American. Web. 04 Nov. 2013.

lion gigabytes) of data. If your brain was a digital video recorder (DVR) it could hold around 300 million hours of television. You better get comfortable with truck loads of your favorite snacks because it'll take more than 300 non-stop years to watch it all. So whether you're a genius or an average joe, your super brain is designed to handle all the stimuli your glory receptors can throw at it.

But wait, there's more. Not only is our super brain able to organize and analyze all that stimuli, but it is able to run self-diagnostics and tune itself up to optimize its performance. In 2006, there was a fourteen-year-old boy named Ben Underwood of Sacramento, California who could use echolocation to find his way around.[19] He was absolutely blind, his eyes were actually artificial, but he made a "clicking" sound to "see" by listening to how the sound waves bounced off objects around him. Yeah, that's how Dare Devil sees, but in real life.[20] Scientist used to think that the visual cortex of blind people shut down but now they know that it rewires itself to "create images" with the information it receives from other senses. Obviously, not all blind people can use echolocation, but all blind people have a brain that rewires itself to amplify other senses. We all do. Our super brain knows if one kind of receptor is failing, or has even completely failed, and will rewire itself to optimize the performance of the other receptors.[21] This phenomenon is known as cross-modal neuroplasticity. This is where our inner worship motor and a standard gas engine from this century start to diverge sharply. Can you imagine a motor in a car that would tune itself up? This self-diagnostic and upgrading feature seems way more like a super power than a mere feat of good

---

[19] "Humans With Amazing Senses." ABC News. ABC News Network. Web. 04 Nov. 2013.

[20] "Dare Devil" - Lee, Stan and Bill Everett. Daredevil #1. Marvel Comics. 1964

[21] "Super Powers for the Blind and Deaf: Scientific American." Super Powers for the Blind and Deaf: Scientific American. Web. 04 Nov. 2013.

engineering. The crazy thing is, it is a standard part of how God designed all of us. God created us with the highest performance worship engines possible.

So on top of all the intricate complexities of how we are hardwired to perceive all the stimuli that floods our glory receptors, is the fact that all those innumerable messages get processed and stored by our super-high capacity, self-optimizing brains. If you want, go ahead and take a second to feel a little super. You are. That being said, please understand that I am not in anyway demeaning or talking down to you or your super brain with this next statement. There is a crucial, though very simple, next step in our foundational understanding of the inner worship engines. So, here it is.

Warning:
You may want someone else to read the following sentence aloud to you so that you might avert your eyes to avoid being blinded by the obvious.

The outcome of our brain processing what we perceive is always the formation of perceptions.

If it makes you feel better, that one was for free. Don't count it in the cost of this book.

The reason this is so key to a foundational understanding of worship is that these perceptions make up our world-view, our understanding of life, our reality. Is the flower that I am seeing beautiful or just another allergen producer? Is my child's diaper smelling clean or dirty? Does this food taste delicious or foul? Is that antique valuable or is it trash? Was that movie good? Was it really that bad? Is that person truly great? Are they secretly weak? These are all answered according to our perceptions. The source of the stimuli, the thing sending stimuli to our glory receptors, is assessed in the formation of our perceptions. This is how our super brain, via neurons, completes the hardwired to perceive function of our worship motors. All the information is processed and stored so that we can form perceptions that in turn form how we see life, the world, and everything in it.

What blows my mind is that our super brain does all of this in real time. There is no drag or need to power up or down to optimize processing speed. It is instantaneous. If you're feeling silly, turn your head to the right and close your eyes. Then turn your head to the left for a different view not held in your short term memory. After five to ten seconds, open your eyes again. Do it now if you want. I don't mind.

Yeah, it all happens that fast. Amazing, I know!

But our super brains are not done yet. As our perceptions are formed, they aren't just logged in our brain as one more entry for that nanosecond. No, our brains do much more. Our brains pull double duty.

Always Responding

Not only are we hardwired to perceive, but we are also rigged to respond. When our brain has formed a perception from all the stimuli, it always responds to that perception. Even when we are being "unresponsive", we are responding to something. Our brain's responses can be as huge as entire paradigm shifts or as insignificant as determining that it is, indeed, time to scratch our nose. Regardless of importance, our brain responds to every perception. How our brain responds, voluntarily as well as involuntarily, is one of the last components of our inner worship engine that will later on give great direction in forming some very practical conclusions. Stay with me a little longer and let's take one last look under the hood.

Involuntary Response

When I first started dating Amber in college, every time I saw her my brain responded. The light would reflect off her and bounce straight into my eye holes to stimulate my optical nerves. My optical nerves would then send a signal to my thalamus (a part of my lower brain) that would send a signal to my visual cortex that would then cue my hypothalamus to release dopamine and norepinephrine into my system. What does this all mean?

Whenever I saw Amber, my brain would basically drug me. Plain and simple. The dopamine causes us to experience pleasure or that feeling of bliss. The norepinephrine makes our heart race and gets us excited. These two chemicals form a cocktail that makes us experience elation, intense energy, sleeplessness, craving, loss of appetite, and focused attention.[22] It has been scientifically proven that recording artist and alleged hobby neurologist, Ke$ha, is absolutely correct in her analytical conclusion that, "Your love, Your love, Your love is my drug".[23] When we are first in love, we are in a very real sense, experiencing a chemically altered reality. The chemicals are all natural, but we are addicts all the same.

All of our super brains are rigged to respond to some perceptions automatically and outside of our own volition. Now, because our responses are automatic, it does not mean that we are all robots. It means that, just like how we are hardwired to perceive automatically, we don't have to turn on a switch or power up or down our ability to respond. There are some specific perceptions that God rigged every one

---

[22] "How Love Works." HowStuffWorks. Web. 04 Nov. 2013.

[23] Ke$ha. Your Love Is My Drug. Animal, RCA. 2010

of us to respond to in the same way. When these perceptions are formed, the response is universal. This isn't a bad thing. This doesn't make you a puppet. This does not make our responses any less real or significant. In fact, like Wolverine's self healing power, involuntary responses are life savers.[24]

When any of us smells food being prepared, our brain fires up our stomach and our mouth starts to water. Because we need oxygen, our brain automatically regulates breathing. When I taste wedding cake and peanuts, my brain registers the deliciousness, so I will eat more to fill the cake-shaped hole we all have in our hearts. But seriously, when I touch a burner and the perception is formed that the burner is too hot, that perception triggers a reflex, and I stop touching the burner before I even consciously understand what just happened. That is a life saver. Or how about when we are startled? That is part of our fight or flight response to danger that makes us ready for action.[25] It is key for our survival. Or what about our "sixth sense", our ability to sense the Holy Spirit? Have you ever experienced a time when you caught a glimpse of God or heard His voice? You get goosebumps. The hair on your neck stands up. Talk about life saving. Our response to God's glory can be a matter of eternal life and death.

Involuntary and even subconscious reactions to our perceptions are an important part of how our brain is rigged to respond. Can you imagine having to consciously tell your heart to beat or the distraction of having to remember to tell your diaphragm to expand your lungs every few seconds so you can breathe? Automatic responses are key to our being able

---

[24] "Wolverine" - Wein, Len and John Romita Sr. The Incredible Hulk #180. Marvel Comics. 1974

[25] "How Fear Works." HowStuffWorks. Web. 04 Nov. 2013.

to even function as people. That includes our ability to function as worshipers.

Voluntary Response

I love Chinese food. I think some of the best things I have ever tasted I tasted when I lived in China. However, sometimes when walking down the streets of China, I would smell what I perceived to be the most revolting food on the planet. It was "chou doufu", which literally translates into "stinky tofu". It is hard to describe its reek without using naughty words. Worse yet, it seemed impossible to know when you might run into one of the billions of roadside stands selling it. Sadly, in those days there was no early warning system. It didn't matter if I was walking through street markets or in front of a major western department store, I was never safe from haplessly strolling into a perfect storm of stink birthed in an unholy union of fermented milk, beef, and bean curd. The sometimes months-old putrescence would fumigate my nose and mouth holes, triggering every one of my 5 million olfactory neurons and 9,000 taste buds. Then my cerebral cortex (the rock star of my higher brain function) would tell me, "Dude, I remember that stink. It is that plague from the very pits of Hell called stinky tofu. A smell so foul it doesn't warrant my learning its proper Chinese name, because then, in some metaphysical way, it would have won."

Then my cerebellum (the key player in my brain's control of motion and coordination) would start my legs and arms pumping in an attempt to flee the culinary crime scene. This would all happen in a matter of seconds. That is, of course, if my medulla oblongata (a first responder in the lower brain) had not already doubled me over to retch. Here's the crazy thing. While I was voluntarily looking for the nearest exit or trash can, there would be Chinese people voluntarily crowding around the roadside vendors, wolfing the briny abomination down like it was cake.

Some run from stinky tofu and others run to stinky tofu. This is because, unlike our involuntary responses, our voluntary responses are not automatic. Voluntary responses are a result of our higher brain functions that enable thinking, emotions, and conscious actions. Also unlike our involuntary responses, our voluntary responses vary greatly. We all automatically respond, but we do not all automatically form the same perceptions about the same stimuli. For instance, some Chinese people would be disgusted by my love of cheese in the same way I am disgusted by their love for stinky tofu. There are some sources of stimuli that we voluntarily respond to very differently. Does this mean our responses can be anything? No. Just like our involuntary responses, our voluntary responses are still steered by our perceptions. Because of my perception that stinky tofu is nasty, I voluntarily respond by avoiding it. Because of some people's perception that stinky tofu is excellent cuisine, they voluntarily consume it. But because of other perceptions besides its taste (like its nutritional value or someone might be holding a gun to my head) I could voluntarily respond by eating it. Those who love stinky tofu could, in the same way, because of other perceptions (like they are allergic to bean curd or they remember they don't like rotten food) could respond by not eating it. Two people can look at the same thing and one think it is beautiful and the other can deem it ugly. I love my wife and believe her to have immense value. To others she is a stranger or even an enemy with very little or no worth. Our perceptions even play out in our response of language. "You like tomato and I like tomahto".[26] Regardless the stinky tofu eater and the stinky tofu hater both voluntarily respond in accordance with their perceptions. That's why when I hear my favorite music

---

[26] Gershwin, I., G. Gershwin, Fred Astaire, and Johnny Green. Let's Call the Whole Thing off. Brunswick. CD.

my super brain tells me, "It's fist pumping time!" And when other people hear their favorite music their brain tells them, "It's two-steppin' time!" or "Let's get our waltz on!"

If you stop and think about it, the world is filled with things that elicit both voluntary and involuntary responses all the time. There are vast opportunities, ideas, and objects that lead us to ponder, feel, and take action. These are all voluntary responses. They are innately tied to our perceptions, but they are voluntary nonetheless. The world is also full of things that create immediate, compulsory responses like sweating, excitement, and even unconsciousness. These are just some of our everyday automatic involuntary responses. All of our responses to anything and everything, both voluntary and involuntary, are due to the fact that we are rigged to respond. Specifically, we are rigged to respond to our perceptions. And the standard in every human hardware that makes up our worship engines is finely tuned to perceive God's glory specifically. We are, in a very real physiological sense, made to perceive God. So what ramifications does this have on our understanding of worship? We're getting ahead of ourselves. There is still more to talk about and understand before we can get to that.

All About Perspective

To make a great comic, everyone knows you need a great hero and a great villain, but even more than those things, you need a great mystery. To drive a compelling story you need a problem for the hero to solve. The hero has to figure out who started the problem.

"How did someone clean out all the greatest treasures of Metro Museum without a single person seeing them?"

"Who poured Chemical X into the city water treatment plant to turn everyone into mindless slaves?"

"How can the hero get through the villain's underground death maze to rescue the damsel in distress?"

Without these questions, these little mysteries that keep us following from panel to panel, there is no story, only a collection of random events.

Every great comic writer knows that the hero's limitations are how we, the reader, identify and connect with these gods among men. And here's why. Even though they have super powers and we are designed with a super brain, we all are limited by our perspective. Both we and the heroes in the comics are never everywhere at once perceiving all the stimuli from all the sources of stimuli at the same time. Even with his super speed and super vision, Superman cannot see what is happening on the opposite side of the planet. Even with our vast array of glory receptors and our super brain, we will never know everything about everything all the time. Just like any gas engine has limitations, so too does our worship engine. One obvious limitation of the gas engine is its dependence on gas. When the gas runs out, it ceases to run. The obvious limitation of our worship engines is our perspective. Even our perceptions about ourselves are limited by our perspective. In Psalm 139, David writes about how God knows the words he is going to say before he even speaks them. David openly acknowledges the mystery involved in even knowing himself from a time-only-moving-forward perspective.

We must take into account the reality of our limited perspectives that consequently limit our perceptions, and thus limit our responses. If we don't, it can wreak havoc on our inner worship workings. Some people can become paralyzed or seemingly frozen in time and space waiting to acquire unattainable certainty. They inevitably settle for the inward facing safety of the little they can perceive. They become closed-minded and trapped by their unacknowledged limitations. Others are rightly able to embrace the mystery caused by their limited perspective and accept the invitation to explore and discover, panel by panel, a larger outward facing story. This is commonly referred to in the Bible as faith.

Of course, being limited in our perspectives is semantic sport with the unimportant or trivial. Sitting down over coffee and jumping through the conversational hoops concerning the fallacies of me claiming Bar-B-Que as my all time favorite food can be a lighthearted waste of an afternoon. Especially since I have yet to taste every single other food on the planet in both time past and future. Smirks over sodas about offhanded declarations of favorites are one thing, but what about the big stuff? What about our relationships with others and God? What about worship or my family or marriage? Am I forever stuck with my current perceptions of my spouse? Do I have to let our relationship just be whatever it's going to be because I will never have all the facts or be able to fully unravel all the mystery that is Amber Pape? Is whatever happens just what happens? No way! I totally work at my marriage and work to know my spouse better. I've spent tons of time with her. In fact, the more time I spend with her in a close, intimate relationship, the more my perceptions of her evolve. As my perceptions of her evolve, the ways my super brain responds to her also evolves. After all these years, my brain now releases not so much dopamine, but instead, endorphins. Endorphins are the body's natural pain killers but they are also soothing and give us a feeling of security. When we first started dating, seeing Amber made me act like I was on crack. This enabled the responses that fostered untiring pursuit. Now, she just has to give me a little reassuring touch and I'm soon more calm and content.[27] As I worked to enhance my perspective via increased time and increased exposure to her, my perceptions and responses changed and matured as well.

---

[27] "How Love Works." HowStuffWorks. Web. 04 Nov. 2013.

Just like there is a kind of work to be done in fostering close relationships, there is also a kind of work to be done in fostering a response of worship. But that is for later. For now, acknowledgment of our limited perspectives moves us closer to our goal of becoming mature worshipers. To become mature worshipers we must understand that the limitations of our perspectives limit our perceptions. This in turn limits our responses of worship. We can never know or perceive everything. So we can either embrace mystery, accept our limitations, and move on in faith and anticipation of discovery, or we will sink ever inward into the madness of endless second-guessing. Faith is not an enhancing element. It is mandatory to become mature worshipers.

Asking The Right Question

All three, Spider-Man, Batman, and Superman have alter egos. When they are off duty, they are Peter Parker, Bruce Wayne, and Clark Kent, respectively. A running tension in all of their stories is keeping their secret identities a secret. Supporting characters are always asking things like "How does Peter Parker always get the newspaper scoop with a perfect picture of Spider-Man?", "How does Clark Kent always miss Superman saving the day?", or "How does Batman always seem to be there when those close to Bruce Wayne are in their most dire need?". These are all good questions, but they are the wrong questions. They assume too much.

Assumptions are our attempt to fill in the holes in our perspectives with guesswork when direct observation via our glory receptors is not possible. Often our assumptions are actually just mis-assumptions in waiting and the questions we form around them lead us to poor conclusions. The greatest mis-assumption in the case of these three heroes is that Peter Parker and Spider-Man, Bruce Wayne and Batman, and especially Clark Kent and Superman are all different people, six separate identities and lives. The "how" questions about each pair of people assumes that the most important perception, that they are two different people, is already settled - even if the only difference is a pair of black framed glasses. This uncreative thinking only fosters unsatisfying answers. Here's a little tip. The best answers to bad questions always feel more like explanations or excuses. As long as the question is based on a weak foundation (mere assumptions), the answers will lead us in circles and to dead ends. This is because assumed reality will always shift or, in some extreme cases, crumble. John Maxwell explains it this way.

"When problem-solving, it's so easy to fall into the rut of uncreative thinking. We can focus so much on answers and solutions that we lose sight of the question. And if we're asking the wrong questions, we'll often end up with the wrong answers."[28]

As the body of Christ, the Church, I think we have been asking the wrong questions. The "How is it that we worship God?" question is guilty of the same fallacy found in the above questions about Spider-Man, Batman, and Superman. Both questions are assuming things about the subjects of their query. To start the conversation concerning worship with "how" questions, specifically assuming God to be the object of worship, leads to answers just as fragile as the assumptions the questions are based upon.

Even if we correct our wrong assumption that God will be the default object of worship, what happens if we only ask "How is it that we worship?" When we only ask "How is it that we worship?", we have a very simple but very unsatisfying answer. We simply receive stimuli via our glory receptors and then respond to that stimuli based on our perception

---

[28] "You Can't Find the Right Answer If You're Asking the Wrong Question." John Maxwell on Leadership RSS. Web. 04 Nov. 2013.

of the source of that stimuli. When our perception of the source of the stimuli is great or worthy enough, our response is worship.

Well, thanks for reading. I guess we're done here.

But seriously, when pressed, we are left with only two very true but very unsatisfying conclusions. The first conclusion is this. We don't have to teach anyone to worship. Everyone naturally does it all the time in accordance with their perceptions. And the second conclusion is as lame as the first. We also don't have to teach anyone how to worship. This is because everyone is hardwired to perceive and rigged to respond to stimuli all the time. Without an on and off switch, everyone worships something all the time. See what I mean? Lame-tastic.

These two conclusions are so unsatisfying because they reveal worship to be natural, unavoidable, and unchangeable by our answering the "how" questions alone. Just knowing how you breathe or how your heart beats or even how you worship doesn't help you do any of them better or even at all. Just knowing the "How it is that they work?" answers alone are TBU (True But Useless).[29] This doesn't mean that when your breathing, heartbeat, or worship stop there is not a serious problem. It is just that only knowing the "hows" of their functions offers no practical course of action.

Don't get me wrong. There is a time and place for the "how" questions. The "how" questions are very important and need to be talked about and wrestled with at the right time. However, there is a question that must be asked first if we are to avoid making the "how" questions our only questions and consequently the wrong questions. The first

---

[29] Heath, Chip, and Dan Heath. Made to Stick: Why Some Ideas Survive and Others Die. New York: Random House, 2007. Print.

question that must proceed the "how" questions is the all time favorite of every small child. The first question is, "Why?".

When you understand the "whys", the "hows" all seem to fall into place. Why are Peter Parker and Spider-Man, Bruce Wayne and Batman, and Clark Kent and Superman never seen together? They are the same people. Once you know that, the "hows" fall into place. The same is true for worship. We have to ask the right "why" question before we get to the right "how" questions if we hope to become mature worshipers of God even if His name is not built into our very first question. The first question to launch a new conversation about worship, the unassuming question, is simply this, "Why do we worship what we worship?". It might help you to read it like this. "Why do we worship X?" Therein lies the rub. This is where the rubber meets the road and we start to build the foundation for conclusions that lead to applications that are anything but TBU.

A Note To Worshipers #3

concerning our uniqueness

Hello again, friend.

I hope the last two chapters have been helpful for you. In the last two chapters we've discussed how we are all the same in some very important ways concerning worship. In light of that, I want to take a second and celebrate how we are all very different and unique despite our common inner worship workings. The fact that God made us unique and different is a huge gift. The more people that experience God from their own unique contextual perspective, the more opportunity there is for us to learn from each other about a God too big for any of us to fully know or experience alone. The various forms that all of the different human worship expressions take are unique responses to unique perspectives of God's goodness and greatness. Sadly, this gift of diversity that allows understanding beyond our own limited perspectives has often been missed because of our obsession with the "How" questions. We shoot ourselves in the foot by automatically rejecting any particular response to God's goodness and greatness due to its manifestation alone.

I'm thankful that God continues to make us all unique despite our missing the point. What would it look like if we asked our Christian brothers or sisters in our ever shrinking world why they respond to God in worship the way that they do, instead of dismissing it as just odd? Imagine how quickly our perception of God would grow with the practice of asking simple questions! How sickening would it be to live life only understanding God from our own limited perspective when we are surrounded by others experiencing the same God in different stories and contexts. Instead, what if we became like God anthropologists, discovering and documenting His effect on the lives of the people He reveals Himself to? All it would take is a little spirit of adventure and a small slice of time to observe or experience another Christ followers' expression of worshiping God. If God is limitless, then we can anticipate God showing Himself to be good and great in a different or new way in the life of every believer!

I'm so glad you've come along on this journey to reveal worship.

Jeremy

A Letter To Worship Leaders - iii
concerning the nightmare carousel

Dear worship leader,

Some of us, including myself, grew up in cultures where we only knew to ask the "how" questions. This was not because we were dumb or uncreative, but because it was the only question modeled for us. Entire churches operate totally unaware that they are asking the same wrong question over and over again. It's like being stuck on some nightmarish carousel. You are stuck with the ups and downs of fads or cursed to ride out meaningless rituals petrified into traditions. You may luck out and get on the right horse for a season or even a few seasons of life. However, the start of the ride is wrought with over-promises because you think you have finally found a new answer to the "how" question and are devastated when it ultimately, totally under-delivers. In the end, just as all the others were, it is exposed to be a choked-out wording of the same old answers to the same old question.

And if that wasn't bad enough - and here's the nightmare part - when you get off that horse you don't get to get off the ride. Because you don't have a better question, you have to pick another horse and ride that one out, bail on the whole thing and hang up your worship leader hat, or become a curator at First "we've always done it this way" Church. I mean, do we need to review the wars fought over robed or business casual? Do we need to rehash the "to drum or not to drum" debates? Are we going to wear our hands raw in just one more reenactment of the traditional vs. contemporary tug of war? Who wants to talk about announcements? Anyone? These have been a series of "how" horses that, outside of the context of the prerequisite "why" questions, have trampled the Church, left a wake of divided losers and vandalized the world's perception of the kingdom of God.

It's time to move on, people. It's time to start asking the right questions and I think you, the worship leader, can lead the way. Start asking "why" questions not with a hidden agenda, but with a real heart of curiosity. Understanding is not elusive but it can require pursuit. It's only when you, our worship leaders, become free from the tyranny of the myopic "how", that we, those you lead, will finally be free to follow you.

I pray strength and perseverance for you.

On behalf of those you lead,

Jeremy Pape

Chapter 2 Discussion Questions

Give an example of when the wrong question kept you or someone else from getting the answers they really needed.

Tell about how a time you and someone else had a different response to the exact same thing.

As you have read about how God designed you, what has been the most inspiring or challenging part for you?

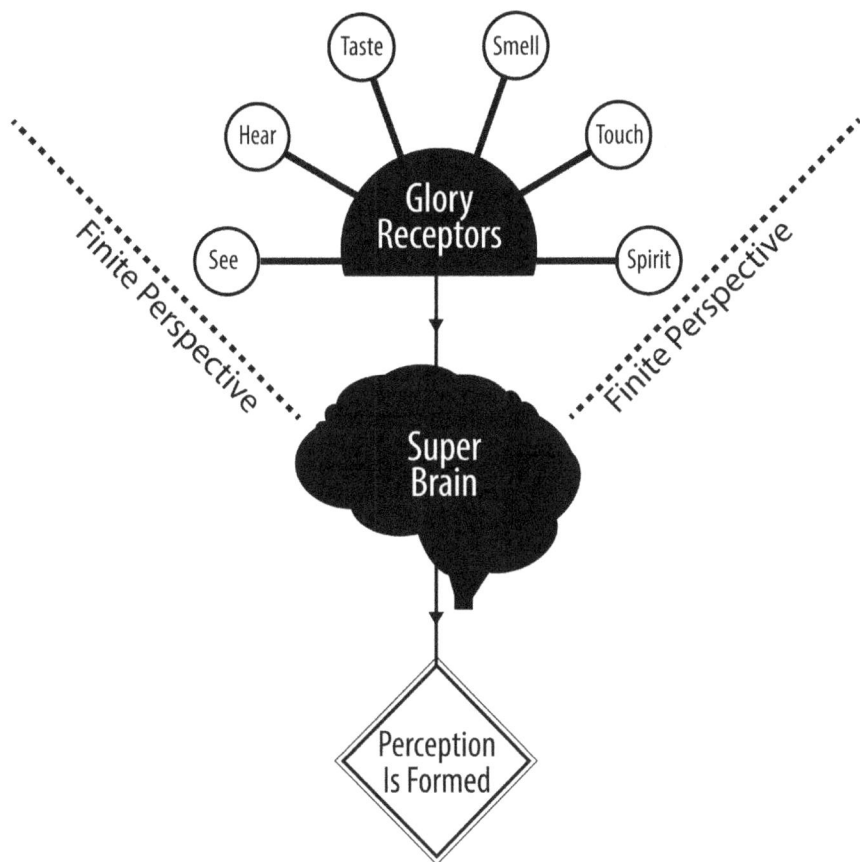

THREE

WORSHIP DEFINED

Noah Webster may not have been a ninja in the literal sense of the word, but if you wanted a spelling butt-kicking, he was your man. In fact, the word "ninja" would have been one of the many words not included in his first publication of the Webster's Dictionary in 1828, An American Dictionary of the English Language.[30] Granted, ol' Noah's been dead for a couple hundred years, but if he were here today, right now, he would give you a grammatical what for.

That's right, my friend.

What. For.

Though void of the word "ninja", the word "butt" was included in Noah's first dictionary publication and defined as everything from vol-

---

30 "1828 Edition of Webster's American Dictionary of the English Language." :: Search the 1828 Noah Webster's Dictionary of the English Language (FREE). Web. 04 Nov. 2013.

umes of beer to ship architecture to door construction to the target of ridicule, but never as one's hind end, backside, or booty.[31]

Mr. Webster spent a good portion of his life on a mission to standardize the spelling and use of the English language. He was successful in a way, but in terms of definitive, exhaustive standardization, not even close. Decades of lexical slang synthesis and the wholesale butchering of foreign language pronunciation has produced shelves full of subsequent editions of that first dictionary and endless fodder for spelling bee moderators. New things and ideas all need new names and terms to describe their new functions. Not to mention the American propensity to casually repurpose all kinds of words to mean things they have never meant before, not excluding or limited to their opposites. I mean, getting soundly bested in a recitative competition of standardized word spellings of increasing difficulty and calling it a "spelling bee" is one thing, but I am literally done using the word "literally" ever again because it is literally never used to mean its literal definition.

Noah Webster knew it, and so do we in the information age. Definitions are very important. Without a common language, the most important word of our question, "Why do we worship what we worship?" is up to the subjective interpretation of well, anyone.

You hardly ever run into a follower of Christ that hasn't at least heard (if not absolutely heart and soul ascribed to) the definition of "love" as stated in 1 Corinthians, chapter 13 of the Bible. In fact, most Christians love confronting the world's definition of "love" by swinging the Bible around like a sword while invoking "Luv Is A Verb" by DC Talk as a battle

---

[31] "1828 Edition of Webster's American Dictionary of the English Language." Search [word: Butt]. Web. 04 Nov. 2013.

cry.[32] If another follower of Christ were to say, "Well, my definition of 'love' is different" or, "Love for me is more like this and that or such and such", they would quickly be rebuked for not submitting to the Holy Scriptures and be seen, at best, as a poor scholar or, at worst, a false prophet.

Ironically, followers of Christ are frequently found saying very similar statements in regards to the term "worship", a term talked about in the very same Bible that talks about love. We have all heard people say things like, "Our worship teams' definition of 'worship' is this or that" or, "Worship to me is when such and such happen together." Unlike the word "love", there seems to be great ambiguity in the use of the word "worship". Why is that? Why is it not okay for us to make up our own definitions of "love" but when it comes to "worship", it's anyone's game? Granted, the Bible states in very plain language "Love is...", but in the absence of such definitive statements concerning worship, do we have the license to choose just any definition or use it in any way that suits our fancy?

The word "worship" seems at times to be so slippery because, like so many of the words in the average English speaker's lexicon, it has been subjected to a myriad of uses. For some reason, we have felt the freedom to repurpose it to our own ends. Though the word "worship" does not carry the reputation of a slang classification, it is treated as such by many Christians all the same. And the crazy thing is, everyone seems to be okay with that.

Let's take a look at some hypothetical definitions of worship based on themes and variations heard around the proverbial Christian water cooler.

---

[32] DC Talk. "Luv Is A Verb" Free At Last. ForeFront, 1992. CD

"Worship is singing to God."

"It's when we find the right posture before God."

"It is sacrificial service."

"Worship is living every moment for God."

"It's a mix of filling your brain up and singing your heart out."

What definition is Biblical? What definition is illogical? Are some really any better than others? Can we even know? I'm no Noah Webster, but the answer is, "Yes, I can." And so can you. Here's why.

Three Givens

As daunting or confusing as the task of defining the term "worship" may seem, we have already discussed all the facts necessary to form a Biblical, logically sound definition. In regards to defining "worship", understanding how we are hardwired to perceive and rigged to respond are definitely "hows" that are anything but TBU. With an understanding of these core components of our worship motors, we can see three crucial truths or givens emerge to provide the proof for an intelligent, unassuming, and Biblical definition of worship. For the duration of the chapter, we will state those three givens, extrapolate a definition of worship, and then clarify and test that definition of worship. So let's get started.

Given #1: People worship different things.

Try not to let your head explode. People worship other things than the living God. I know, crazy! I'm being facetious, but this is a key truth in our understanding of worship. People perceive the same concept, person or thing (including Stinky Tofu), to have differing degrees of worth. So one thing perceived to be of great worth to one person may be perceived as worthless by another. The Bible and countless years of recorded human history shows that people worship other things besides God all the time, regardless of having all the facts. If my definition of the term "worship" intrinsically includes or assumes God as its focal object, then either the Bible is lying or my definition needs work.

I'm going to defer to the Bible on this one.

Any good definition of worship cannot, in itself, reference any specific object or focus of worship. If we are to honestly embrace the realities of idolatry, we cannot include God or any manifestations as Father, Son, or Holy Spirit in our definition of worship. You cannot include the object of worship in a Biblical or logical definition of the term "worship" because people worship different things.

Given #2: Worship is a natural response to what we perceive.

It's natural for me to go crazy at a game winning touchdown or while my favorite artist performs their hit song. The style or expression of worship is different from person to person, but it is a natural response, in whatever form, for everyone. Because we are rigged to respond and we always respond either voluntarily or involuntarily to our perceptions, we can conclude that worship, a response, will be automatic or flow naturally from one who perceives something to be worthy of it. As we talked about before, we do not need to tell anyone to worship or to teach them how to worship, because we are rigged to respond. It will happen naturally. One possible response is worship. Worship is a natural response to what we perceive.

Given #3: Everyone worships something all the time.

Because we cannot turn off our ability to perceive, to form perceptions, and in turn, to form our responses, we are always perceiving something to be of greater worth than all other things and thus responding to that something with worship. In our formation of perceptions, we assess the worth of the source of the stimuli perceived. Is it good? Is it great? Our running tab of perceptions deeming what things are best, worst, greatest, or least is why we have favorites. What are you fixated on? What draws and holds your attention as something more important than anything else? What do you draw life from? What has the greatest weight in your decision making? Everyone has answers to these questions and the answers point to the object of our worship. People worship something all the time. We do not start it or stop it. Thus, if we place conditional statements regarding time and place to our definition of worship, we are again refusing to accept the realities of the world in which we live. The woman at the well in John 4:20 throws Jesus a curve ball concerning time and place when she asks "Our ancestors worshiped on this mountain, but you Jews claim that the place where we must worship is in Jerusalem." Definitions of worship contingent on time or place are falling prey to a classic and, understandably, typical mistake, but a mistake nonetheless. We are hardwired to perceive all the time and rigged to respond all the time and thus are always worshiping something all the time regardless of when or where we find ourselves.

Testing Definitions

Here again are the three givens.

People worship different things.

Worship is a natural response to what we perceive.

Everyone worships something all the time.

These givens allow us to confidently detect false definitions and seek a true definition of worship. They are invaluable and extremely clarifying when used to test any possible definition of worship. Let's run some of the previous, hypothetical definitions of "worship" against our three Biblically and logically sound givens.

"It's when we find the right posture before God."

This definition breaks all three givens. It includes the object of worship in the definition ("God"). It assumes a specific kind of response ("right posture" - whatever that is). And the third strike is its time condition ("when"), implying that there are times that one is not worshiping. Three strikes and you're out. This cannot be the definition of worship.

"It is sacrificial service."

This one is a little better in that it's simple, but worse in that its one and only statement is false, thus making it devoid of any truth at all. It is demanding that everyone's expression of worship (a natural response steered by our perceptions and perspectives) always takes the form of sacrificial service. Maybe sometimes. But all the time? I don't think so.

"Worship is living every moment for God."

This one at least acknowledges given number #3 in its timeless nature. However, someone's act of worship might be to die for God. For example, Jesus Christ. And that's not to mention the countless terrorists or cult members that have died in worship to someone or something other than God. No, this definition, like the others, leaves us unsatisfied. Here's one more.

"It's a mix of filling your brain up and singing your heart out."

I'm tempted to simply dismiss this one for its abandonment of conventional wisdom concerning the oil-and-water nature of term definition and the use of euphemisms. Any euphemism, not to mention two in the same definition, only add confusion to any kind of definitive study. This is not to say that I might not steal it in a narrative description of a particular response of worship, but it is a poor definition - not to mention it breaks given #2.

So, where does this leave us? Is worship undefinable? Some have resigned to declaring it so. Honestly, without the foundation that we have spent the last few chapters constructing, I would agree. Definitions that are merely derived from our own worship expressions are actually descriptors of our volitional practices of worship, rather than the literal definition of the term. I have no problem with people describing their own propensities for a specific practice or favorite ritual. The real problems arise when those descriptions or practices become surrogate definitions of the actual term. However, in light of our conversation thus far, I'd have to say "worship" is absolutely definable. Using the three givens, we have a working map for navigating the storm to safely arrive at a definition of worship that is both honoring to God's design of us and the Biblical handling of the term.

Defining Worship

Just as a solid understanding of the working parts of a gas engine can make a simple diagram seemingly draw itself, we will attempt to achieve similar results by piecing together the basic parts or givens concerning worship. I believe the following definition both embraces and allows for authenticity in people's relationship or non-relationship with God without assumptions. This definition also acknowledges very real physiological and psychological realities consistent with the truth; that we are all created beings living in a created world, who perceive and respond to God's glory as revealed through the Bible. So here it is.

```
"Worship"
(wər-ship) - verb
The natural human response to anything of
greatest perceived worth
```

Not too fancy. Straight to the point. Let's take a quick look at the construction of this definition and then put it under the same scrutiny as the previous definitions by holding it up to the light of our three worship givens.

The

The word "The" implies that this definition is the only option, not that it might be one of the options. It's like the "the" in "the fall of man" or "the resurrection of Jesus Christ". All of them are definitive and all are designated as such by the inclusion of the word "the".

Natural

The adjective "natural" means that whatever follows is not contrived or synthesized. "Natural blonde" and "Natural athlete" are examples of this use. It flows or happens automatically. There is no on or off switch. Worship is not faked or even able to be faked.

Human

The inclusion of "human" is needed because we are not talking about or concerned with just any animal or plant or mineral of any other part of creation. It is also all-inclusive in that if you are human, you share this same trait with all other humans. If you are a human being, this definition applies to you. If you are any other kind of animal, or a mineral, or a plant, HOLY CRACKERS, YOU CAN READ!

Response

The noun "response" is the subject of our definition. It is naming worship as a response, an action birthed from our being hardwired to perceive and rigged to respond in accordance with our perspective. It is not specific in its expression, but it is elicited by something.

To

The word "to" indicates there is a source of the stimuli eliciting the response. Without this word, for instance the use of "in", "with", or even "from" in its place, the definition takes on a very different meaning. A meaning not conducive to the truths we have uncovered thus far.

Anything

Nothing is excluded. The word "anything" leaves no room for predetermined or assumed objects of worship. The focus of worship is not limited to only red things, blue things, old things, or new things. It can be any and all things. Anything. There are no limits to what can be worshiped, physically or metaphysically.

Of

The word "of" is small yet crucial, just like the word "to". It tells us what qualifications are required for the specific response of worship to manifest. "Of" signals that a condition has been met. A certain perception must exist to trigger the response of worship.

Greatest

The adjective "greatest" firmly fixes the issue of greatness as settled. There is nothing more great. The ultimate of great has been obtained. It is not moderately so. It is not tied with. It is not on par with. It is supreme in its degree. There is no other greater.

Perceived

The word "perceived" holds all the connotations of the previous two chapters of this book. We form perceptions limited by our perspective that result in the aforementioned response. We are hardwired to perceive. There is no turning it on or off. Our perceptions include the assessment of the source of the stimuli. This all happens regardless of our accuracy in determining actual reality.

Worth

The word "worth" implies an assessment has been made. The object's quality of value or merit has been ascertained. Worth is a judgment of how deserving or costly an action or object is. It can be low or high. It has no innate benchmark. "Worth" is a condition of an object dependent on the perception of the object.

Testing Our Definition

So how does this collection of words, this definition of the term "worship", stand up against the three givens of worship?

"Worship is the natural human response to anything of greatest perceived worth."

Given #1 - People worship different things. This given is satisfied with the words "anything" and "human". There is no predetermined object or focus of worship.

Given #2 - Worship is a natural response to what we perceive. The second given is satisfied with the words "natural", "response", "to", "of", "perceived", and "worth". It incorporates all God has revealed concerning the workings of those he has created to worship.

Given #3 - Everyone worships something all the time. The third and last given is satisfied by the words "The", "human", and "worth". The definition is timeless and devoid of people group classification.

Even more, a good definition won't leave you with a handful, or sometimes a truckload, of "except whens". What about if someone is physically unable to sing or kneel? What if someone likes drums and someone likes bagpipes? What if there is no music whatsoever? What if it happens outside on a mountaintop or in a tiny dorm room? What if it's toward an idol instead of the living God? All of these can be understood in the context of this definition. There are no exceptions to be made. The definition is solid and thus what we build on it will also be solid. This includes our most anticipated applications.

So, let me pull out the ol' trail map and point out how far we've come and where we are going. We are chock full of glory receptors. These glory receptors perceive stimuli including, most importantly, God's glory. They then send signals to our super brain. Our super brain then catalogs and stores the information to form perceptions of the source of stimuli. This is all because we are hardwired to perceive. But our brain is not done yet. We then respond both voluntarily and involuntarily to our perceptions. This is all because we are rigged to respond. Additionally, the range of stimuli we perceive is limited by our perspectives, thus limiting our formation of perceptions, and in turn steering our responses. All of this points us to three truths or givens concerning our inner worship workings.
People worship different things.
Worship is a natural response to what we perceive.
Everyone worships something all the time.

We know that we don't need to teach people to worship or teach them how to worship, but instead we must explore the question of "Why do we worship what we worship?" But before we can answer the million dollar question, we have to define the most important term in our question, "worship". So we defined "worship" as the natural human response to anything of greatest perceived worth. This is how far we've come. We've covered quite a bit of ground.

Noah Webster defines the word "revealed" as disclosed; discovered; made known; laid open.[33] I think we have taken a good long look at our inner worship workings and can, with a clear conscience, declare "worship" to be revealed. Worship is not magic, but a very real function that we are designed and equipped to perform.

So, are we done here? Is that it?

No, my friend, there is still much more to talk about, as you have probably surmised by the remaining number of pages to your right or the progress percentage indicated on your e-reader. Knowing how a motor works and even being able to produce a simple diagram of all the working parts is one thing, but driving a car to a specific destination, namely being wholehearted worshipers of God in spirit and truth as described by Jesus in John 14, requires us to journey a little longer together. It's like we've come over a hill and are able to see an extended view of the rest of our journey. In the distance we can see our mountain top destination but there is a valley to cross first. That valley is filled with the problem of God's position of greatest worth clashing with our limited perceptions, and the consequences of that contradiction. We have to cross through the middle of this valley to get to the other side; a giant "X" marking where we find application treasure for our lives as followers of Christ. So catch your breath, let these last few chapters sink in and in the next chapter we'll start our descent into the issues surrounding being a natural responder with limited perspective and being a follower of Christ; i.e. the Disciple's Dilemma.

---

[33] "1828 Edition of Webster's American Dictionary of the English Language." Search [word: Revealed]. Web. 04 Nov. 2013.

A Note To Worshipers #4

concerning how we use the word "worship"

Hi,

So I'm super stoked that so many of us are talking about how to define the term "worship" instead of just throwing it around willy-nilly. Words are so important to us. They contain entire concepts. Defining the important words in our lives can create the paths we need to get to even higher concepts. Defining the term "worship" puts us well on our way to be the worshipers both we and God want us to be. For me, it can be so frustrating to be in a conversation where others are throwing around words that I don't understand, or in ways that don't fit the context I'm used to. It makes me feel like such an outsider. I don't want myself or anyone to feel like an outsider when it comes to worship, and neither does the God that lovingly created us. Sometimes it only takes one new definition or context clue to open up the whole conversation for us. As people passionate about seriously following the Lord Jesus, we will spend the rest of our lives learning. I hope this new definition of "worship" opens up the conversation of your own journey in new and exciting ways.

For the time being, let's agree to make how we talk about worship accessible to anyone by being mindful of the context in which we use the term "worship". We may even have to offer the definition on needed occasions. I am a verbal processor, so this goes double for me. Let's all agree to give our mouths the buffer time required to keep our super brains from abusing or repurposing the term "worship". K?

Your friend,

Jeremy

A Letter To Worship Leaders - iv

concerning the context in which you use the term "worship"

Dear Worship Architect,

I humbly and respectfully ask you to thoughtfully consider how you talk about worship, especially in how it pertains to the worship of God. Please, no more absolute statements about what the response should look like. No more talking about worship as if it automatically means you are responding to the living God. In the best case scenarios, I would call these declarative, flagrant opinions a party foul - "poor scholarship!". In the worst case scenarios, situations including people leading others in their arrogant "redefining" of what God has made seen, I would cry "charlatan!"

This chapter contains one definition. I think it's pretty awesome. I'm not demanding that you buy into it wholesale. I hope you do. However, whatever definition you land on, don't sabotage the chances of those you lead to embrace that definition by casually throwing it around as a shorthand for concepts it was never meant to describe. Sing-alongs and lectures can be found in all kinds of non-worship settings including everything from Cub Scout meetings to lynchings.

But besides just being more careful of what we say, we can also be purposeful in helping others talk about worship. It's sometimes hard to know how to respond when someone comes up to us and says something like, "you really brought the worship today!". I think we all know to at least say, "Thanks". That is sometimes all we have time to say. But sometimes we have a minute, and if we can have the presence of mind to ask them, "What part of God's goodness or greatness did you respond to?" then we can really help lead that person to begin to understand what worship is all about without subjecting them to a five minute mini-sermon.

Thank you for your leadership and for your faithfulness. Thank you for your teachable spirit even if you don't fully agree with all that I've said. That, more than any definition I have to offer, is what will keep you in the game for the long haul to serve the dear people in your circles of influence.

Blessings,

Jeremy Pape

Chapter 3 Discussion Questions

Describe a time you have had a complete miscommunication due to the misunderstanding of a word's meaning.

On a scale of one to ten, how important is wording or word use to you?

What are some other definitions of the word "worship"? How do they stand up against the three worship givens outlined in this chapter?
1. People worship different things.
2. Worship is a natural response to what we perceive.
3. Everyone worships something all the time.

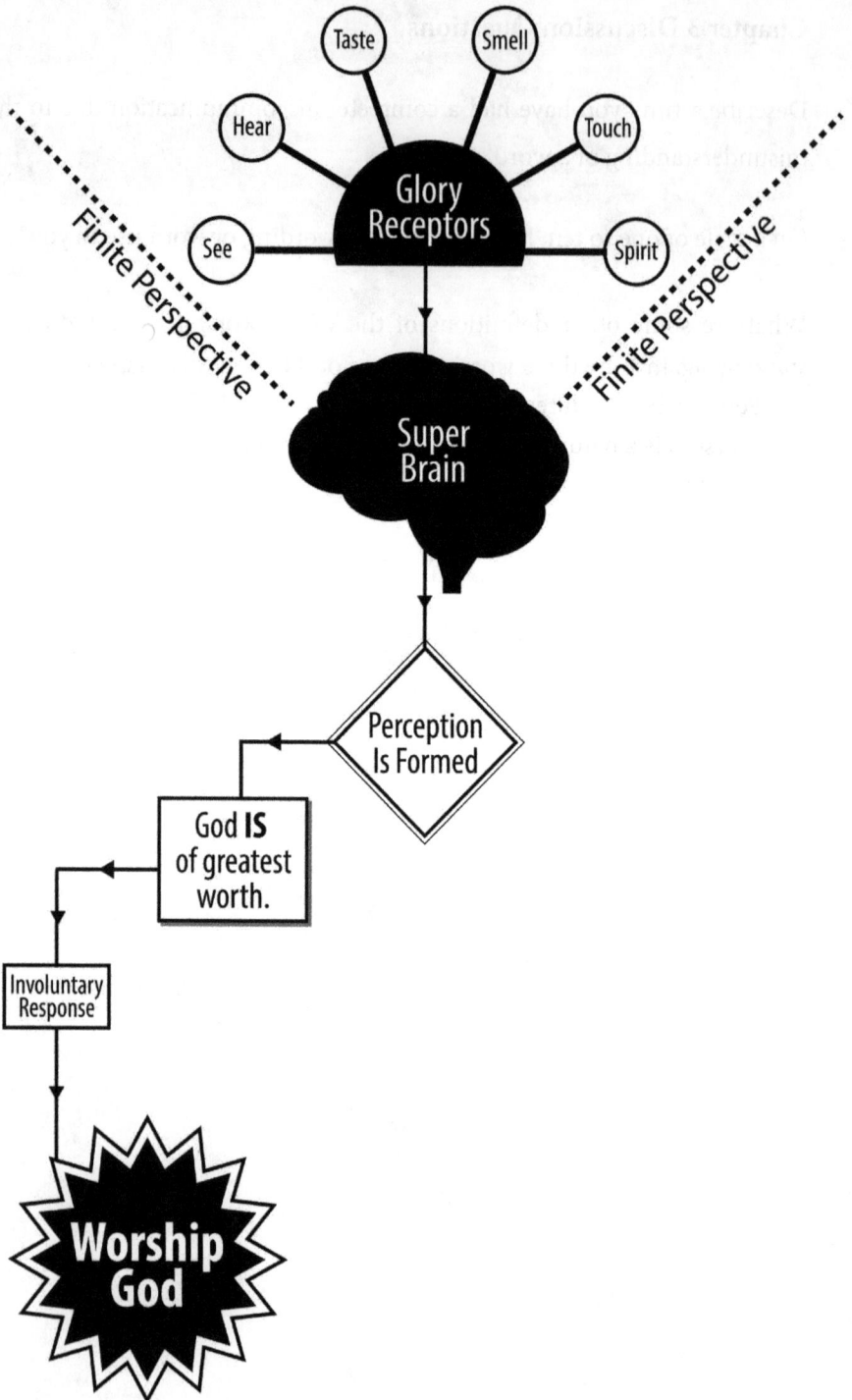

FOUR

THE DISCIPLE'S DILEMMA

Not too many Sundays ago, I awoke too early after too little sleep. Difficulty turning off my mind once it's started, plus having a highly people-orientated profession equals being an old friend with insomnia. For me, insomnia is like Kramer on Seinfeld.[34] You never know when it will show up, but when it does, you know there is no quick fix and you'll probably end up visiting the fridge before it's over.

Anyway, resigned to wakefulness, I got up and soon found myself ready to make my 8:00am pre-service rehearsal call time with plenty of time to kill. So, throwing the Sunday comics and that week's advertisement inserts onto the passenger side seat, I drove to a gas station just down the road from the church building for the breakfast of Atkin's champions - Jerky and Diet Mountain Dew.[35] Loitering outside the gas station like some sort of get-away car didn't seem like a good option, so I pulled my

---

[34] "Seinfeld - Official Site." Seinfeld - Official Site. Web. 04 Nov. 2013.

[35] "Low Carb Diet Program and Weight Loss Plan I Atkins." Low Carb Diet Program and Weight Loss Plan I Atkins. Web. 04 Nov. 2013.

car into the outer-rim territories of the Wal-mart parking lot down the street to enjoy my paper, a little music on the radio, and my no-carb soda and two-carb jerky in peace.[36]

After making short order of both the food and the ads, it didn't take long sitting in the parking lot of a store brandishing the delineation, "Super Center", for a pattern to begin to unfold in my mind. "Unfold" is wrong. Maybe, hit me like a truck. The church facility I was getting ready to serve in and the store had much in common, and not just the exterior masonry style both had adopted to fit in with the look of the surrounding commercial architecture. Both places had large accommodating parking lots and wide welcoming doorways to optimally serve the masses. Both openly offered something to those who entered whether it was low prices, the Gospel, or a mix of both. Upon entering either one, you would be greeted by people who didn't know your name, but it wouldn't be creepy because they'd all wear large name tags. Both places found people crowding in around the holidays and both places made claims about the importance they should hold in the everyday lives of the American people and their American dreams. The similarities were a trifle unnerving, if not disturbing. Of course, in many ways, there were glaring differences, but one thing was undeniable. They were both places of worship. I even had the full page, four-color scriptures of the retail gods laying neatly beside me on the passenger side. The whole experience played out in a relatively short amount of time, but it is a moment burned into my memory; its lesson not to be forgotten nor its irony to be missed.

So, why am I telling you about this particular bout with insomnia and the object lesson that ensued? To help prepare you for your mid-book quiz. In the world of higher learning we have mid-terms. This is your

---

[36] "Wikia." Wookieepedia. Web. 04 Nov. 2013. The outer rim territories are the boondocks of the Star Wars universe.

mid-book. No peeking at your neighbor's paper. It's only two questions and true or false questions at that. You may start…now!

Mid Book Quiz
True or False

1. ___ We are all made to worship God. *(50pts)*
2. ___ We all naturally worship God. *(50pts)*

I'm not with you so you'll have to grade the test yourself. As you mark your score, remember God is omnipresent and think about W.W.J.D. - what would Jesus dock.

Answer Key

1. *True* - The statement "We are all made to worship God" is true. See chapters 2 and 3 of this book.

2. *False* - The statement "We all naturally worship God" is false and is counter to everything we have talked about thus far, including what the Bible reveals about worship.

Armed with a good definition of worship (the natural human response to anything of greatest perceived worth), we can now answer the million dollar question, "Why do we worship what we worship?".

Here it is. The fruit of our journey thus far. Are you ready?

We worship the thing we worship because we perceive it to be of greatest worth.

We may not have all the facts. But as far as we know, all our perceptions, both conscious and unconscious, stack up and point to the object or focus of our worship to have the greatest worth. There is nothing else greater or more good in our world-view than whatever it is that elicits the response of worship from us. There it is. That is why we worship what we worship.

It's hard to put into words how big this is. It's really everything. If any one of the three givens that helped us define worship weren't true, if all people worshiped only God or perceived only God to be of ultimate worth, or worshiped only when they perceived God to be of ultimate worth, that would be one thing. However that is not the case.

For Christ followers, this just got real.

Worship Only God All The Time

Obviously, as followers of Christ, as disciples of Jesus, our propensity to worship so many other things besides the living God poses a huge dilemma. Some of us tend to worship our career, 401k, and upward mobility. Others worship artists and celebrities or knowing the latest gossip about them. Some people joke about their worship of coffee, but challenge their devotion and you will soon see attitudes and actions proving it to be anything but a joke. Reputation, body type, and fashion seem to be teen favorites. Who can fit the most in their dump truck-sized shopping cart and throw it all away in six months seems to be a favorite ritual of young adults. Some parents worship their children. There are a faithful few worshipers of social media still holding onto the weathered ruins of Myspace but most have converted to the tenants of Facebook.[37] Christians sometimes even worship their worship leaders, songs, or even a particular form of worship. Even the conceptualization of the term "worship" in book form can become an object of worship.

We were made, even exclusively and painstakingly designed, to worship God. However, getting every Christian to effortlessly worship only God is not as simple as just sitting back and letting nature take its course. To jump to that conclusion is, at best, naive, and at worst, dangerously negligent. Let me tell you why.

---

[37] "Myspace." Wikipedia. Wikimedia Foundation, 11 Mar. 2013. Web. 04 Nov. 2013.
"Facebook." Wikipedia. Wikimedia Foundation, 11 Mar. 2013. Web. 04 Nov. 2013.

God is not cool with us only getting the focus of our worship right sometimes. He wants and deserves ALL our worship ALL the time. In Exodus God tells the people, "You must not have any other god but me. You shall not make for yourself an idol in the form of anything in heaven above or on the earth beneath or in the waters below".[38] In Matthew, Jesus Christ himself commands, "You must love the Lord your God with all your heart, all your soul, and all your mind. This is the first and greatest commandment".[39] It's not a suggestion. It's a command. Disciples are commanded to worship God and only God and it seems that this particular command gives no regard to our leanings, the cultural pressures towards idolatry, or our limited perspectives. To worship anything or anyone other than God is to break God's commands and an attempt to make life work apart from Him. Simply put, it is sin and there are real consequences of that sin for us. Some consequences are immediate and others more subtle but all are dangerous. Here's an example.

The Danger

Once upon a time, a long, long time ago in a place far, far away there lived a little slave boy and his mother. One day, two very kind and powerful men along with some traveling companions rescued the boy from slavery and took him to many far away places on many great adventures. One of the companions of the two men was a young girl, and the boy soon fell head over heels in love with her. Although it took many years, he eventually discovered that she also loved him and so they were married, but not without complications. First of all, the boy was engaged in strict training to become like the two men who had previously rescued him from slavery. He was to become an agent of goodness and power to

---

[38] "Exodus 20:3-4." The Holy Bible: New International Version. Grand Rapids, MI: Zondervan, 2005. Print.

[39] "Matthew 22:37-38." The Holy Bible: New International Version. Grand Rapids, MI: Zondervan, 2005. Print.

protect those in need. This was a complication because the station and classification to which he aspired required absolute abstinence from developing deep, personal relational attachments. This was so that he could be free to administer impartial justice. Similarly, at the same time the boy was training, the girl had become an important public servant. Their love was birthed in both secret and scandal but it still grew and flourished.

Ah, forbidden love.

It was not long after their secret marriage that the boy began to have dreams of the girl, the love of his life, calling out to him as she was dying. This greatly bothered the boy because similar nightmares had previously haunted him concerning his mother only a short time before her tragic death. So the boy set out to do whatever it took to save his love from what he perceived to be her impending doom. This impossible end, stopping death's hand from taking away those he loved, so consumed the boy that, in its name, he betrayed the very men who had originally emancipated him from slavery, descended to become an agent for evil, and ultimately assaulted   his young bride and their unborn twins. The pursuit of the power to control death became the single greatest thing in his world-view, the primary focus in his life. It became even more important than those he was hoping to protect in the first place. In the end, he gave himself and everything else over to his obsession and lost everything, including himself.

Obi-Wan Kenobi puts it this way to young Luke Skywalker. "The Jedi were the guardians of peace and justice in the Old Republic. Before the dark times - before the Empire...a young Jedi named Darth Vader, who was a pupil of mine until he turned to evil, helped the Empire hunt down and destroy the Jedi Knights. He betrayed and murdered your father. Now the Jedi are all but extinct. Vader was seduced by the Dark Side of the Force."[40]

This struggle for control over the uncontrollable, for relief from fear, and the resulting destruction is sadly common. Despite the fact that Darth Vader's story is a piece of fiction, our definition of worship can still be applied seamlessly and the story's warning still be relevant to us.[41] God does not command us to worship Him alone all the time to control us, but for our own good. Given time, we eventually give ourselves over to our focus of worship. We all have seen people give their entire lives over to things not worthy of human devotion. It is often messy and not very pretty. Families fall apart. Priorities are skewed. Addictions are formed. Lives are marked with serious regret. It is catastrophically damaging and malignantly toxic to our lives if our focus of worship is anything other than the one true God. This is as true for followers of Christ as it is for unbelievers. Jeremiah warns, "They followed worthless idols and became worthless themselves."[42] I like the New American Standard Bible translation better. It reads, "And walked after emptiness and became empty."[43] Moses warns the people before entering into the promised land that "If you ever forget the LORD your God and follow other gods and worship and bow down to them, I testify against you today that you will surely be destroyed."[44] God does not need our worship. His position as the one of

---

[40] Star Wars. Twentieth-Century Fox Corp., 1977.

[41] "Darth Vader." Wikipedia. Wikimedia Foundation, 11 Apr. 2013. Web. 04 Nov. 2013.

[42] "Jeremiah 2:5." The Holy Bible: New International Version. Grand Rapids, MI: Zondervan, 2005. Print.

[43] "Jeremiah 2:5." New American Standard Bible. La Habra, CA: Foundation Publications, for the Lockman Foundation, 1971. Print.

[44] "Deuteronomy 8:19." The Holy Bible: New International Version. Grand Rapids, MI: Zondervan, 2005. Print.

greatest worth is complete and unchallenged regardless of how we perceive Him. No, it is we who need to worship God and God alone. To not do so is to expect to be seduced and destroyed by the dark side.

How Did This Happen?

So, if worship of other things besides the living God is so prevalent and so dangerous, the following questions beg to be answered. If we were made to worship God, what happened? How did we come to live in a world where everyone, including ourselves, so often misperceives God's irrefutable position of greatest worth? If God created everything, how could we miss it? How could anything supplant the goodness and greatness of God in our world-view?

To understand how one arrives at a particular destination, you must follow them from their point of origin. Then the pattern becomes clear. So let me take you back to our origin, so we can come to see the way in which we find ourselves here today; people made to worship God, but not worshiping God.

"In the beginning, God created the heavens and the earth" (The Book of Genesis, chapter one, verse one). After setting the stage, God created mankind, namely Adam and Eve. Adam and Eve knew God and loved God. The goodness and greatness of God was in full display, clear as day and as close as the nose on your face. The man and woman were made to worship God and they did.

But then Satan, God's fallen enemy, approached the man and the woman and asked a question. "Did God really say 'You must not eat from any tree in the garden'?"

The woman, Eve, replied, "We can eat from any tree in the garden. But God did say, 'Don't eat from the Tree of the Knowledge of Good and Evil that is in the middle of the garden, don't even touch it, or you will die.'"

To which Satan replied, "You will not certainly die, for God knows that when you eat from it your eyes will be opened, and you will be like God, knowing good and evil."

And for the first time, Eve questioned her perception of what had the greatest worth. God claimed to be (and was) of greatest worth. Satan claimed knowledge of good and evil to be (though it was not) of greatest worth. There were then two things competing for Adam and Eve's worship. Conflict had now entered the story. The conflict of two truth claims. The story in Genesis continues.

Eve saw that the fruit of the tree was good for food and pleasing to the eye. The stimuli produced by the fruit was received by Eve's glory receptors in her eye. The nerve impulses traveled to her super brain where they were processed and cataloged to form a perception; "Dang, that fruit looks good!" The Bible does not tell us how she came to believe Satan's claim concerning the fruit. It does show her response, thus making it clear that her perception of God and the fruit from the tree of the knowledge of good and evil had switched places and switched in a moment. Eve's perceptions changed and her volitional response christened the beginning of the end. The following six words relate one of the darkest hours in recorded human history,

"She took some and ate it."[45]

---

[45] "Genesis 3:6." The Holy Bible: New International Version. Grand Rapids, MI: Zondervan, 2005. Print.

Despite God flooding her every glory receptor with His glory, Eve chose a lie over the truth. She came to think that God was holding out on her by keeping her from the knowledge of good and evil. Knowledge is power and we know now, just like Eve figured then, that power is a vehicle for control. Eve chose control over trusting God because she perceived it to be of greater worth than God. Adam, passively watching the whole thing go down with the intervention initiative of a couch stain, also took some of the fruit and ate it. He chose the path of least resistance. Adam chose relief. Both Adam and Eve were co-responsible to follow the instructions of God to not eat of the fruit and they both sinned against God.

Just as we do today, they both quickly came to understand how false the promise of control and relief offered by Satan was. They were ashamed and probably would do anything to call a mulligan and take a do-over shot, but alas, the damage had been done. The continuous response of worship from Adam and Eve to God, if even just for an instant, had been choked off and diverted from the creator to the created. It sent the man, the woman, and the rest of human history spiraling. Eve was to obey her husband (goodbye control) and Adam would spend the rest of his days in toil (nice knowing you relief). Their children and their children's children and on and on through all the generations would follow suit. Today we follow a pattern of mis-perceiving things other than God to be of greatest worth and worshiping everything but the very one we were created to worship.

This is our origin story. This is how we find ourselves in a world filled with beings made to worship God but worshiping everything else instead. Paul sums it up this way in Romans; "They exchanged the truth about God for a lie, and worshiped and served created things rather than the Creator".[46] It is Adam and Eve's story and it is our story.

Self-Worship

What part do we play in this story? In all of creation, there is one created thing that especially competes for our worship. Go look in the mirror if you want to take a look at it. That's right. It's you, the one holding this book right now! Well, not just you. It's all of us. We are most tempted to worship ourselves. It's most apparent when we observe our greatest motivators and highest standards to be measured by statements like "convenience for me", "comfort for me", and "safety for me." When our actions show that we perceive ourselves, our wants, or our needs to be of greatest worth, it is a short path to discern the origin that led us to this place. The root is basic egocentricity, which is just a two dollar word for self-worship. It is we, ourselves, that are the greatest contenders for the title of most worthy against the awesome, incontestable goodness and greatness of God. It's a battle that, in reality, we always lose. However, we are beings with limited perspectives and have a real knack for pushing our capacity to be dead wrong to its absolute limit.

Not only is self-worship the idol of choice in our day, but it is also the most celebrated and reinforced. We see it in everything from rewarding "whatever-it-takes-to-be-number-one" attitudes to very subtle undercurrents in questions like "What do YOU want to get a degree in?", "What ways do YOU want to better yourself?" or "What does God want YOU to do with YOUR life?" We may not actually go to churches with pictures of ourselves in stained glass but self-worship is the true secret faith and the most-practiced religion of men and women in this, our post-fall world. Its sacraments are control and relief, and its sanctuary, scorning

---

[46] "Romans 1:2." The Holy Bible: New International Version. Grand Rapids, MI: Zondervan, 2005. Print.

our limited perspectives, is the naive claim to have grasped the whole of knowledge, including the knowledge of good and evil.

Jesus' Quiz

One day, a couple thousand years ago in the first century, Jesus took his disciples to a place about twenty-five miles north of the sea of Galilee for a little field trip. The area they went to was near Caesarea Philippi, a hotbed of pagan worship to the half-man, half-goat god, Pan.[47] They were surrounded not only by an idol-worshiping culture, but also by a society with a polytheist view. This was all totally foreign to the disciples. They had all grown up in a monotheistic culture. They were not in Kansas anymore and they knew it. It is in this context that Jesus asked his disciples a simple question with a boatload of implications. And what does he ask? Does he ask how the disciples are going to choose to keep following God when everyone else is worshiping goat boy? No. Does he ask them to pinky swear to never come back to this or any other place that promotes a different belief system? No. Does he ask them how they will worship him in a culturally relevant way in the midst of a culture rife with immorality that would make Hugh Heffner blush?[48] No. Jesus gives them a pop quiz with two questions. His are not true and false. They are short answer questions. Here is the quiz Jesus gave his disciples.

Identity Quiz

Short Answer

1. Who do they say I am? *(0pts)*
2. Who do you say I am? *(100pts)*

---

[47] "Caesarea Philippi." (BiblePlaces.com). Web. 04 Nov. 2013.

[48] "Hugh Hefner Biography." Bio.com. A&E Networks Television. Web. 04 Nov. 2013.

Jesus asked them, "Who do people say that I am?".

The disciples replied that some people perceived him to be John the Baptist or Elijah, maybe even Jeremiah or one of the prophets.

Jesus then asked them, "But what about you? Who do you say I am?"

Jesus knew that their perception of him would take care of all the "how" questions of worship. By asking the "who" question, Jesus was getting to the heart of "why".

Simon answered, "You are the Messiah, the Son of the living God."

Jesus told Simon that he had answered correctly and then proceeded to change Simon's name to Peter. Jesus went on to say that upon this foundation, this rock, the truth of who Christ was (and is), the Church would be built and the gates of Hades would not stand against it.[49]

Jesus knew that if the question, "why do we worship what we worship?", was answered, then the rest of the questions and answers would have a rock-solid foundation to stand on. As followers of Christ, we share Peter's confession that Jesus is the Christ, the son of the living God. It is to this God, (The Father, Son, and Spirit), that we are lovingly commanded to worship regardless of our circumstance. We either worship only God all the time or we worship anything else in disobedience and sin. The question is this. "How do we worship only God all the time?" I know that focusing on the "hows" or a particular expression of worship won't help. I also know that worship is a natural human response to anything of greatest perceived worth and my perspective and perceptions can be so easily skewed.

---

[49] "Matthew 16:13-18." The Holy Bible: New International Version. Grand Rapids, MI: Zondervan, 2005. Print.

So let's get out the ol' trail map one more time and let me point out the two possible paths we are faced with. In the next two chapters we will take a look at both paths. I'll start with the not-so-good choice because I am most familiar with it. It is the path of pretending and faking. It actually turns out to just run in circles. The second path is the path that leads straight to some real skills and practices to humbly navigate the Disciple's Dilemma. It is the way to wonder.

A Note To Worshipers #5
concerning when we find ourselves steeped in idolatry

Hello again, fellow worshiper.

I know the mandate to worship only God all the time can seem over-whelming - especially when it seems so easy to worship just about anything on any given day. Here's the good news. Misdirected worship of other things is often just a few clicks off of worship of God. God is a perfect father who fully knows and celebrates us. We were designed with the desires to be seen, loved, and enjoyed. This is not so that we would struggle with self-worship or the worship of anything else promising those desires, but to fully depend on and find them fulfilled in and by God. God promises Heaven where all our needs and desires will be fulfilled forever. Jesus modeled a kingdom here on Earth where we are offered hors d'oeuvres of this via authentic, Christ-centered community. When we find we are worshiping something other than God, the first step is not self-condemnation, but instead, thanking God for the insight into our own hearts and, second, redirecting our worship to be on God. How do we do that? That is what we are getting to. I can't wait to talk about it. It's coming up in the next chapters.

I'm so glad you are on this journey with me.

Yours,

Jeremy

A Letter To Worship Leaders - v
concerning redirection of the wandering-eyed worshiper

Dear dot connector,

I'm sure I don't have to tell you how easy it is for the people you lead to check out at a moment's notice or physically show up but never fully engage in a response of worship to the Living God. At least people are showing up. That means you get a few moments to try to redirect their attention away from all the distractions and back to God's goodness and greatness. That doesn't mean you have to ignore the tragedy or minimize the biggest news so that everyone can focus on God. Instead it might be a matter of one or two dots that need to be connected for people to find God in the tragedy or big news that has captured their attention. A few words putting everything in context of God's goodness and greatness can be all the help those you are leading need. Your task is not to try and fool people into thinking everything besides God is no big deal, but rather, via as few connecting points as possible, help them see what a big deal God is. God has done more than his part in being good enough and big enough to fully inspire our inner worship engines. Our energies are thus best spent perfecting our skill and mastering the craft of being astute dot connectors. We want to lead people back to God in as few steps as possible.

Here's a free hint. The fewest steps or dots connecting back to God lead right through the tragedies and big news of their lives, not around.

I hope you are being blessed by this book. Even if you think I'm crazy, I'm glad you're thinking about this stuff. Again, I am praying for you and only want the best for you. I hope you hear that.

Sincerely,

Jeremy Pape

Chapter 4 Discussion Questions

Tell about a time you saw someone become obsessed with or overtaken by the thing they worshiped.

What would you add to the list of things you see people worshiping?

How does being or not being a follower of Christ affect how you pursue worship?

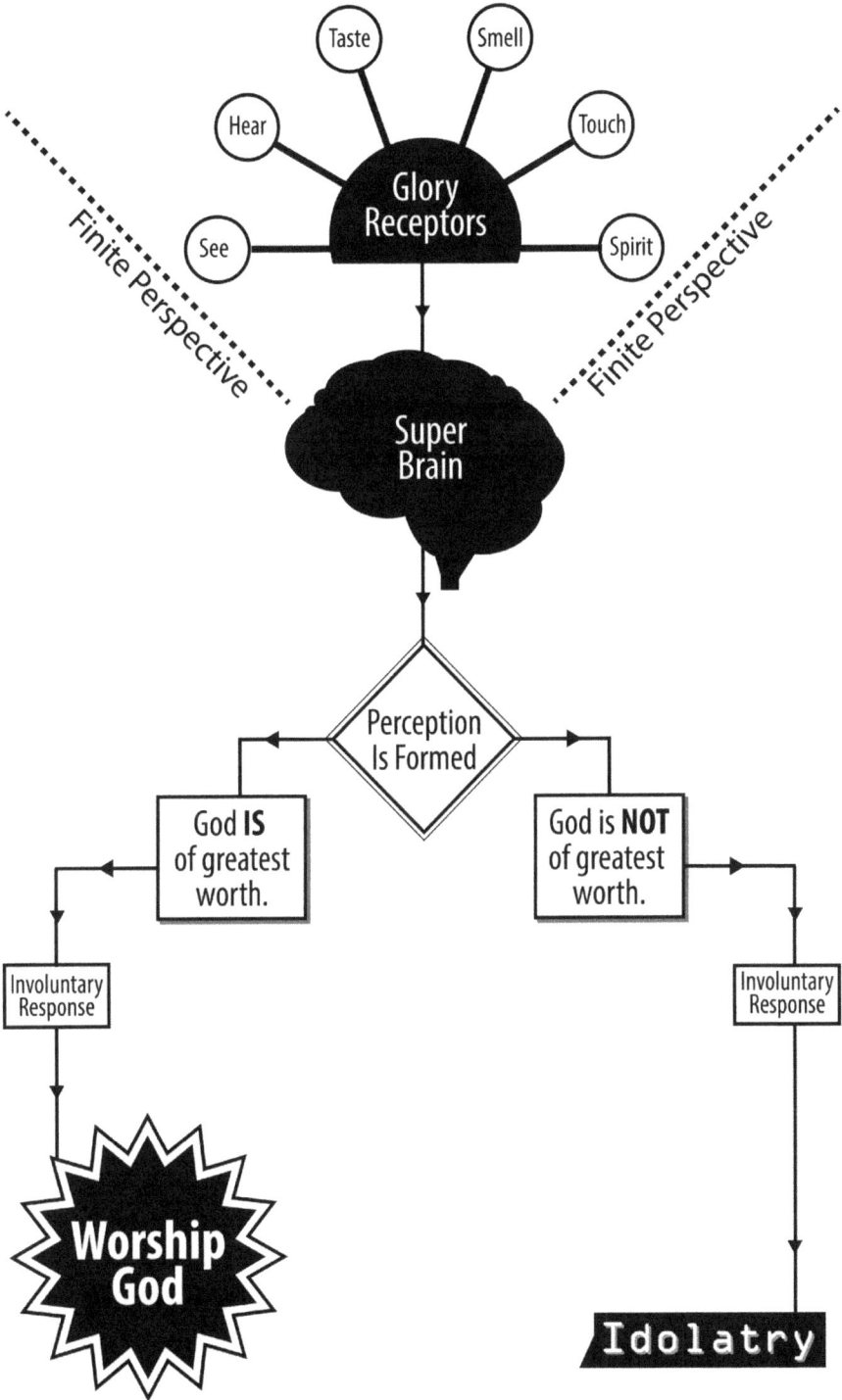

FIVE

THE FAKER'S FOLLY

Have you ever found yourself in a large group worship gathering and for some reason you were just not "into it"? Or have you sneaked a peek around and felt like just another face going through the motions? Or have you ever felt like a giant spiritual vacuum was used to suck all the energy out of a room, making you feel less like you are sharing in the movement of God and more like you are showing up to fulfill a duty. I know I have. I think we all have. And it's in these moments that one of my greatest fears for the church starts to rise up into my throat and make the hair stand up on the back of my neck. That's right. Zombie attack!

Just think about it. There are people shuffling or swaying listlessly from side to side making mindless vocalizations with a hungry look in their eyes before lunch. I'm not insinuating that the people around us might be zombies, but if zombies did covertly infiltrate our corporate expression of worship and shuffle in from the back, we might not know until it was too late. That's why I sit near the front.

Seriously though, I'm not trying to prop one expression of worship up over another, especially by merit of observable enthusiasm. We are all unique. What I am trying to say is that we all have been in situations that had been especially designed to help us worship only God all the time but there we stood (or sat or knelt) simmering in just how much we didn't feel like worshiping. We all have endured times when we knew we should be, but for some reason, were not that excited about God. Even more, sometimes I've felt distant or angry with God in those situations. There are also those times when I finally get away to spend time alone in private worship but I end up thinking about, well, everything else.

You may not be distracted by your fear of zombies, but we all can be distracted. It might be your late car payment or your wayward child. You might be wondering if your drive home will be a continuation of the argument you had with your spouse this morning. Regardless, life is full of situations and circumstances that capture our attention and imprison our passions. What do we do with that? How do we steer our focus and attentions through the choppy waters of life? What can we do when we carve out time to intentionally respond to the living, all-powerful God of creation but we have, as the Righteous Brothers put it, "lost that loving feeling. Now it's gone, gone, gone, whoooooh"?[50]

As I mentioned in the last chapter, there are two possible paths. There may be many side trails of the paths, but when you look at the big picture, all the themes and variations coalesce into two basic modes of action in pursuit of fostering a natural human response of worship to the living God. One path leads to frustrated disappointment and the other to God-honoring results. One way requires a good amount of fatalistic denial, the other a good amount of intentional work. One route leads to un-

---

[50] The Righteous Brothers. "You've Lost That Lovin' Feelin'". You've Lost That Lovin' Feelin'. Philles 1964

healthy performance and the other to a healthy, authentic response. In this chapter, we'll take a look at the first path, the way that I believe is not very fruitful in regards to inspiring an authentic response of worship to God. Then in the next chapter we will describe the more healthy path; one that I believe is able to foster a natural human response of worship to God. This is partly because I want to show the more positive way in light of some of the more common pitfalls along the road to authentic worship, but also because, to be honest, I am all too familiar with said pitfalls. My hope is that my past failures will smooth the way for your future success. I'm not claiming that after familiarizing yourself with these two paths that you will never stumble again. Instead, I hope and pray that when you do find yourself down in the worship dumps, you will be able to pursue a new route that leads to real results in dealing with the Disciples Dilemma. Remember, the command we are given is to worship only God all the time. So let's take a look at the first path, the path of the faker. Albeit the path of a well-intentioned faker, they are a faker nonetheless.

An Unfortunate Conversation

Let me start by offering a simple but common dialogue. Most of us have heard a form or variation of it in our communities of Christ followers.

CHRIST FOLLOWER #1
Just worship God.

CHRIST FOLLOWER #2
I can't "just" worship God. No one "just" worships God.

CHRIST FOLLOWER #1
We were made to worship!

CHRIST FOLLOWER #2
I really, really want to but it's just not coming right now.

CHRIST FOLLOWER #1
Lame.

CHRIST FOLLOWER #2
Totally.

We've all been there. We confess that despite the appearance of everyone around us "feeling it" today, we are having a hard time connecting to
God's goodness and greatness and our response to Him is anything but
worship. Then someone tries to help us by encouraging us with the truth
that we are made to worship, but they are wrongly insinuating that this
means we should automatically worship God. Remember the Mid-Book
Test in the previous chapter? And then, because we don't have a solid
foundational understanding of how God designed us to worship, we are
hit - BAM! - with an overwhelming sense of powerlessness and
hopelessness. We start to put two and two together.

"If God never changes and everyone else in the room is worshiping,
then it's probably something wrong with me."

That kind of condemnation never feels good so we protect ourselves by
retreating into cynicism or fronting an image of "worshipy" countenance
or activity. Both are unhealthy. Both are following the path of the faker.

(Oh, snap! Did I just write that? Cynics are fakers? Man, paint me con-
victed.)

But seriously, the cynic is faking hidden knowledge about the "How" questions. The mimic is faking actions that resemble the "How do we worship" responses being expressed by the majority of those around them. Both the cynic and the mimic want to have a response of worship to a specific object. They both want to believe the object is of greatest worth. But they simply do not perceive that object to be so. But what other option is there? We assume we must fake it.

Isaiah 29:13 gives us one of the clearest peeks into God's feelings concerning fakers. The Lord says, "These people come near to me with their mouth and honor me with their lips, but their hearts are far from me. Their worship of me is based on merely human rules they have been taught."[51] The way of the faker is the way of the person who goes through the motions without reason. It is the way of the person who says all the right things even if they don't understand or believe them.

This truth begs me to address a common heresy. There is a phrase thrown around among Christ followers frustrated with not having that loving feeling. It is the advice to "Fake it 'til you make it." Rather than going into how this is antithetical to all we have talked about thus far and taking it apart bit by bit, I want to address this with a quick but poignant axiom. I tried to think of a way to address this false teaching in a way that is both honoring to God AND readable by my mother, but then I remembered all the times God just laid correction out through His prophets. For what it's worth, I'll only use language already found in the Bible. So here it is. This is my axiom concerning the "Fake it 'til you make it." false teaching.

Even whores orgasm sometimes.

---

[51] "Isaiah 29:13." The Holy Bible: New International Version. Grand Rapids, MI: Zondervan, 2005. Print.

There it is. You're welcome.

Cause And Effect

Honestly, I believed for a long time if I followed this teaching, to just fake it long enough, it would eventually feel real. I used to hope that the music or performance would sweep me away. I fell into the "Fake it 'til you make it" practice, believing the rush or high must be worship. But in my euphoria, was I really worshiping God or sharing a response with others to some event, a dynamic leader, or even music itself? I was wrong and so are those that are still trying to get different results (worshiping only God all the time) by implementing the same methods (show up and pretend).

I hope as followers of Christ we never intentionally set out to be fakers or are ever truly satisfied with faking it. But without a solid, foundational understanding of our inner worship workings, being a faker is really the only path available. I know it was for me. Unfortunately, despite any ignorance of an alternate path, we cannot fake it or just really, really want to worship God, and here's why. It is because of a two cold, hard truths.

IF our perceptions = GOD > X, THEN we will worship GOD.
IF our perceptions = GOD < X, THEN we will not worship GOD.

The constant and natural human response to God being of greatest perceived worth is always worship of God. The constant and natural human response to God not being of greatest worth is always not worship of God. If I believe God is of greatest worth, I will respond in worship to God. If something else is at the top of the list or holds the position of greatest worth, I will worship it instead. Whatever it is, an idea, an object, or anything at all, if it is what I perceive to be of greatest worth, I WILL worship it instead of anything else, including God.

Let me put it this way. The value (greatness of worth) you perceive something to possess (regardless of truth) directly relates to the intensity and passion of your response (to worship or not to worship) to that focus. When we truly perceive God's glory, we can't help but worship him. If we do not perceive God's glory, we will not worship Him. In the same way, if we are not worshiping God, it is simply because we do not perceive Him to be of greatest worth. If we worship something besides God, it is because we perceive it to be of greater worth than God.

It may seem black and white, but don't let this truth discourage you. It is actually very helpful in freeing us from the tyranny of just trying harder to want it more. And to be honest, God totally stacked the deck in His favor. He made us with the capacity to worship anything, but not without supersaturating the humanly perceivable and even imperceivable (the microscopic and telescopic) universe with every possible ounce of His glory. It wasn't until 1990 that we first saw the images from the Hubble Telescope. Who knows what is still waiting to be discovered to add to the symphony of stimuli flooding our glory receptors? God taunts us to seek it out and bask in its source.

We Can't Fool Ourselves

Another key concept that exposes the folly of the faker is that we are incapable of consciously tricking ourselves into assessing something to be of greatest worth when we are clearly perceiving it not to be so. Trying to do so is like a magician trying to trick himself with the same magic trick he is performing for others. We can't just short circuit how we are hardwired to perceive and rigged to respond in hopes of tricking our super brains into worshiping God instead of something else. We cannot form a perception and then just will ourselves to perceive reality in another way. If this were the case, we could just tell ourselves how to think, feel, believe, and behave and we would. All of the counseling, psychological study, and psychiatric practice in the world would all be for naught and we could all go about our Utopian, controlled, skinny lives.

For example, imagine we go to an exclusive garage in the poshest part of the city and you ask me to compare two vehicles. One is a little red push wagon and the other is the 2012 Lamborghini Gallardo Lp 570-4 Spyder Performante.[52] I cannot stare long enough or look from just the right angle to ever will my super brain into believing the wagon to be of greater worth than the sports car. One is a clunky, "push-it-up-the-hill-yourself", fifty dollar, cast-iron toy while the other sports a high perform-ance 5.2-liter V10 engine that produces 570 horsepower all packaged in the most elegant, mechanical luxury materials. Each Lamborghini is a near miraculous feat of engineering and priced at around $240,000.00 a pop. No matter how much I pretend, I can't look at a shack and go through enough mental gymnastics to believe it to be of greater worth than a royal castle.

When we try to fool ourselves, intentionally working against God's de-sign for us to function as worshipers, we really become a kind of worship zombie. It also reveals some fallacies in the ways we understand God. God is the master mechanic, the premier designer, the preeminent engineer of our inner worship engines. Do we trust that His goodness and greatness has birthed in us the form optimal for our worship func-tion, or is our energy best used to bypass or fool it? Who are we to try and circumvent how God designed us? Going through the motions even when we do not perceive God to be of greatest worth is not only fool-ish, but counterproductive to our desired response of worship. How could we ever truly worship a God that we were able to correct or play for a fool?

---

[52] "2012 Lamborghini Gallardo LP 570-4 Spyder Performante." Top Speed RSS. Web. 04 Nov. 2013.

Not only is being a faker counterproductive in our pursuit to make God the object of greatest perceived worth, but God is totally NOT cool with it. In the book of Amos, God has some pretty choice words to say to a bunch of fakers going through the motions. "I hate, I despise your religious festivals; your assemblies are a stench to me. Even though you bring me burnt offerings and grain offerings, I will not accept them. Though you bring choice fellowship offerings, I will have no regard for them. Away with the noise of your songs! I will not listen to the music of your harps."[53] There's nothing more offensive to a God who hardwired us to perceive and rigged us to respond to His glory than for us to just show up and fake it. He infused the universe with stimuli so that we would worship the one and only, the very creator of all things, the ultimate in goodness, the epitome of greatness, God himself. Not only can we not really fool ourselves into worshiping God, but it is an insult to God to try.

We Can Be Fooled

Conversely, as impossible as it is for us to fool ourselves, it seems to be alarmingly easy for us to be fooled by another. This is why I love magic tricks. We can definitely be fooled. Have you ever looked at an optical illusion? We are hardwired to perceive, rigged to respond, and equipped with a super brain, but that doesn't change the fact that when I look at M.C. Esher's "Ascending and Descending", featuring a seemingly never ending staircase, that I am suckered for a moment into thinking that those little people are going to be walking up and down those stairs for - ev - er.[54] Granted, I quickly decipher the illusion after further inspection. Nonetheless, that does not diminish the fact that I was momentarily fooled. And after all, a moment is all it takes. Advertisers know this better than anyone.

---

[53] "Amos 5:21-23." The Holy Bible: New International Version. Grand Rapids, MI: Zondervan, 2005. Print.

[54] "Ascending and Descending." Wikipedia. Wikimedia Foundation, 11 Jan. 2013. Web. 04 Nov. 2013.

Think about billboards, television, and radio ads. "This car will make you happy." "This house is worth anything to buy it." "This product will make you popular." "This activity will make you lovable." We are repeatedly bombarded with objects or ideas promising enhanced self-worship. No matter how much these pale in comparison to God in reality, after enough unchallenged prolonged exposure, we can be fooled into thinking that they just might be of greatest worth - if only for a moment. And if we start to fill limited perspectives with these things in the effort to better our illusion of control or relief, they can actually start to be perceived as being of greater worth than God. The results can last for more than mere moments. Sometimes our perceptions are changed for a season or even a lifetime.

We cannot fool ourselves, but we can be fooled. There are many who tirelessly labor to make us perceive either they themselves or what they are offering is of greatest worth. Whether it's the promise of popularity, happiness, a dream, being seen, being loved, being enjoyed,or anything else, there are those who wish to fool you. If we are practicing fakers, we are already predisposed to accepting comfortable lies over cold and hard truths.

In light of the foundation we have built for being a thinking worshiper, the conclusion to our little unfortunate conversation might play out like this.

CHRIST FOLLOWER #1
Why won't you just worship God?

CHRIST FOLLOWER #2

> I can't just worship God even if I really,
> really want to because I don't really, really be-
> lieve God is of greatest worth.

God Mis-perceptions

If we are not really, really believing God to be of greatest worth, then how are we perceiving Him? If our journey to be worshipers of the living God starts off with a view of God other than how He reveals Himself in the Bible, then we have little hope of ever being more than a faker. We can't just get pumped up enough to trick ourselves into ascribing the position of greatest worth to a misinterpretation or a caricature of God. This is a common though typically undetected pitfall. Let's take a look at a few common caricatures of God.

Take for instance the ever popular "Officer God". When great tragedy hits, when space shuttles crash, and when trade towers fall, we are glad to see him. When we are speeding or trying to get away with something, we watch out for him or are even a little scared of him. Otherwise, "Officer God" is mostly out of sight, out of mind. How could we honestly worship this god? We can't.

Or what about "Santa God"? We can be tricked into thinking of God like Santa Clause when we find ourselves in a season of life in which blessing after blessing seems to be pouring down on us. We feel like it's Christmas all the time. Everything is going well. We may actually be having our very best life right now. But when the party is over, when it appears that the steady flow of prosperity has been choked off, there are real grounds to put "Santa God" on trial and get to the bottom of what's causing the lag in the frequency of your blessings. Is God visiting other people first and running out before he gets to you? Are the elf angels on strike? What is it? And what about real tragedy? If God's first job is to bless us, then he must be distant and apathetic to allow bad things to happen to good people. How could we honestly worship "Santa God"? We can't.

As a worship leader, I can accidentally point people to worship "Fido God". "Fido God" is the best pet you will ever have. He's small and desperate for your love. His tail shakes uncontrollably and he barks like crazy when you show up to religious stuff. When you toss him the occasional bone of good deeds or prayer he practically wets himself. "Fido God" is very manageable, if not at least house trained. How could we honestly worship this god? We can't.

A tragically common caricature of God is the "Personal Trainer God". He is looking for people to help, but first they need to help themselves. He's waiting for people to meet him halfway or at least really try to come as far as they can. He'll work with you and even make you strong and powerful but you better be ready to get up before the sun and sweat that sin right out of your soul. "Trainer God" is a brutal task master that offers a grace with strings attached. How could we honestly worship this god? We can't.

The list could go on and on. These and the myriad of other misinterpretations of God can render any authentic worship response to the living God of the Bible impossible. Understanding only a caricature or a piecemeal God can only lead us into folly. If we only worship the parts of God's character that we like or want Him to have, then we have, in a very real sense, placed ourselves above Him and are right back into self-worship. Don't mess around with this. Call it what it is, stop it, and let's keep going.

So in conclusion, we will never be able to ramp up our emotions or find the perfect environment in which we can fake our way back to that loving feeling. Thankfully, the band Boston reminds us that it's about "more than a feeling".[55] It's about perception. And even though it's all too easy for our perceptions to be skewed, there is real hope. We do not have to be worship fakers or worship zombies. We are ready to look at the more healthy path; the path that leads to an authentic response of worship to God. Exactly how do we pursue a natural human response to God being of greatest worth without falling into the faker's folly? Hold onto your hats. That's coming next.

---

[55] Boston. "More Than A Feeling". Boston, EPIC. 1976

Note To Worshipers #6
concerning zombie survival

Hey,

So you don't want to be a worship zombie, huh? Well, knowing is half the battle. Here are the two biggest warning lights that indicate you or someone you love is on the slippery slope to becoming a worship zombie.

Warning Light #1
Zombies are lazy. They take the path of least resistance and have a hard time navigating closed doors. They will never give the little bit of energy it might take to pry open a window to their own soul to let in more of God's goodness or open a door of their heart to reflect on God's greatness. This is because they want everything to just, you know, flow from the Spirit. They are happy to participate and sing along without giving any thought to what's going on. They forget that Spirit-led does not mean Spirit-done.

Warning Light #2
Zombies are expert consumers. Their identities and days are defined by what they consume and the rate at which they consume. They are laser-focused on the gratification of brain gobbling or the ecstasy of mountain-top worship experiences. They are alive on the outside but dead on the inside, so they are forced to keep consuming the life of events and activities, only to keep moving on to the next event or activity. Wash, rinse, and repeat.

So, if you observe any of these symptoms in yourself or in others, the best course of action is to just exterminate them right there on the spot. Just kidding. Seriously though, you don't want to play around. You've got to take responsibility and action to make sure everyone gets the help they need *to move toward repentance and restoration. First steps might look like a well-asked question or even a Biblical call to honor God in everything we do. Do not let these symptoms go unchecked, especially in your own life.*

If you keep your eyes open, you can safely navigate your way through the hordes to a place of authentic, life-giving worship.

Jeremy

A Letter To Worship Leaders - vi

concerning "thar be other monsters about."

Dear worship leader,

Sometimes I really pity you. Here you are, called by God and charged to lead me in corporate worship, working your tail off to draw my attention to the world-rocking goodness and greatness of God, and what am I doing? I'm lookin' for zombies. I'm not sure what's worse though, my spiritual Attention Deficit Disorder or my Mr. Hyde-esque transformations into a scathing cynic.[56] I could stand there forever judging from my back row, ivory tower; crossing my arms and burning holes through the frozen smiles of your band with my death-ray eyes and apathetic jaw waging. It's hard to say which is the real monster threat, zombies or me? Zombies won't write e-mails, they just keep shuffling along.

Despite any concern with zombies or fear of being waylaid by my sinful, fallen, cynical nature, you and I both have an additional, and dare I say, greater common enemy to fear. The monster we leaders must join forces to fight is the dreaded doppelganger. A doppelganger is a monster that looks like us but is actually a demon in disguise. Our doppelganger wants those we lead to be happy with something I call "the worshiper's high". The monster lets those he or she is called to serve treat them like magical rock stars in exchange for paltry parlor tricks and mere musical entertainment. Matthew 5:16 commands us to "Let your light shine before men and glorify God in Heaven."[57] The greatest tragedy would be for us to let our doppelganger go unchecked and to let peoples' fixation with

---

[56] Stevenson, Robert Louis., and Rosemary Border. The Strange Case of Dr Jekyll and Mr Hyde. Oxford: Oxford UP, 2008. Print.

[57] "Matthew 5:16." The Holy Bible: New International Version. Grand Rapids, MI: Zondervan, 2005. Print.

our doppelganger go unchallenged. The result is people worshiping our spotlight instead of being blown away by the goodness and greatness of God. So let's grab our pitchforks and our torches and hunt that monster down. Hopefully, because of our conversation thus far and with the tools offered in the next chapter, we will equip ourselves and others to do exactly that.

Happy Hunting,

Jeremy Pape

Chapter 5 Discussion Questions

Describe a time when you just weren't "feeling it" in terms of worshiping God.

What do you see people turning to most often for the feeling of control or relief?

What are some other God mis-perceptions or caricatures of God not mentioned in this chapter?

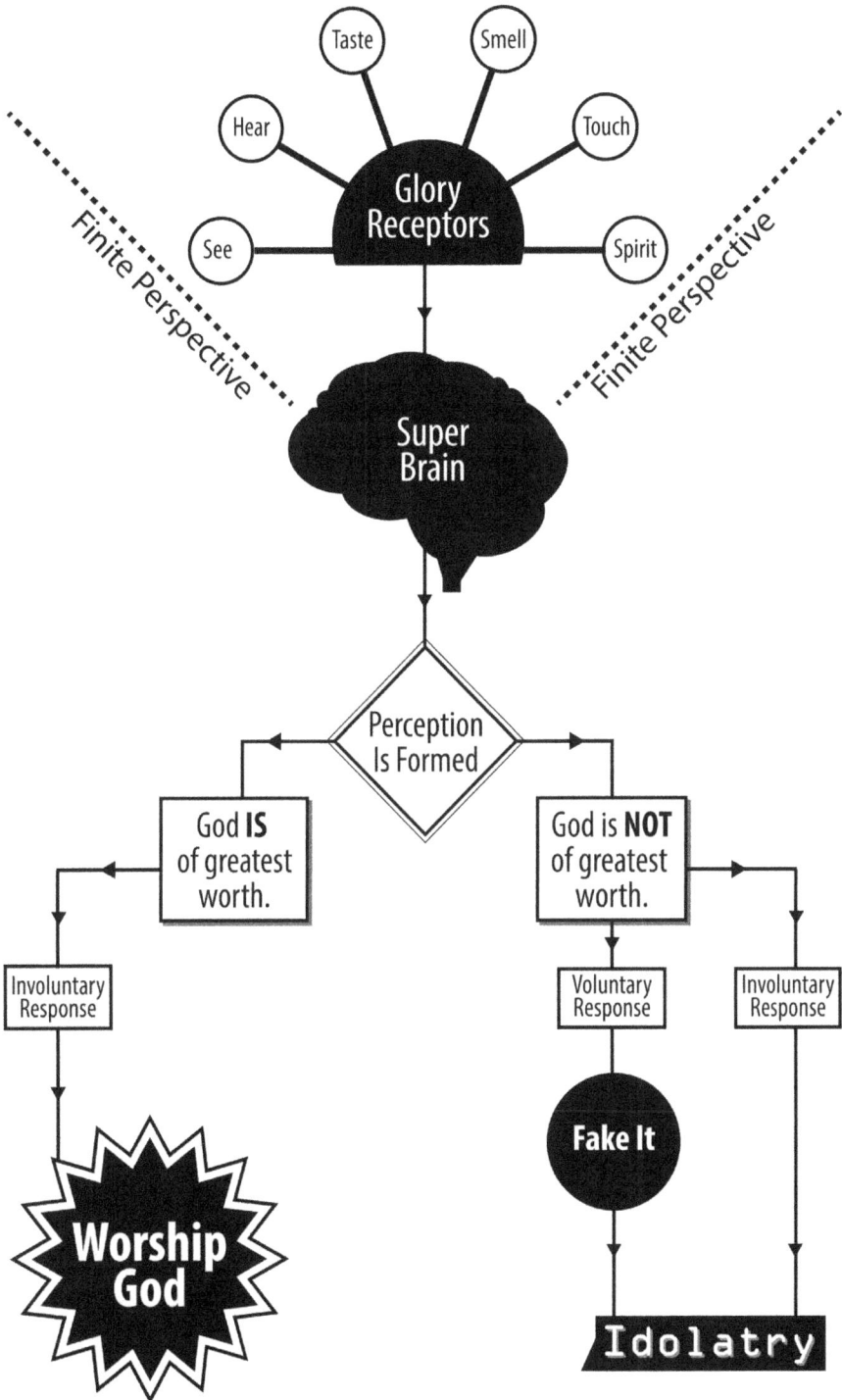

Taste

Smell

Hear

Touch

Glory
Receptors

See

Spirit

Finite Perspective

Finite Perspective

Super
Brain

Perception
Is Formed

God **IS**
of greatest
worth.

God is **NOT**
of greatest
worth.

Involuntary
Response

Voluntary
Response

Involuntary
Response

Worship
God

Fake It

Idolatry

SIX

WORKING TOWARD WONDER

We started our conversation on worship by talking about how worship is not some magic trick. It can and should be revealed. We have looked at our own inner worship workings to see the form and framework in which our God-designed purpose of worship can function. We've put in the legwork to grasp and understand a definition of worship that is both God honoring and rooted in the realities concerning His design. We have taken the Disciple's Dilemma seriously and have even identified and dismissed the way of the faker. There is still work to be done. We have a little farther to go. It is now time to step out confident in the solid theological and logical foundation of worship we have laid. In these last few steps of our journey together, we are not working to gain bragging rights or self-aggrandizement. We are striving to worship the living, creator God. We are working toward wonder.

In the previous chapter, I cited Isaiah 29:13 as one of God's indictments against worship fakers. Let's take another look at Isaiah 29:13 and the verse directly following it to see what God plans on doing in response to the peoples' fakery.

13 The Lord says:

"These people come near to me with their mouth

   and honor me with their lips,

   but their hearts are far from me.

Their worship of me

   is based on merely human rules they have been taught.

14 Therefore once more I will astound these people

   with *wonder upon wonder*;

the wisdom of the wise will perish,

   the intelligence of the intelligent will vanish."[58]

(*Emphasis added*)

God's remedy for the faker is not to put them on a hand raising workout or a Christian Radio diet. Tragically, these would only serve to enhance the faker's "fakerness". Instead, God will once more blow them away with wonder upon wonder. Praise God that wonder has never been contingent on fully understanding or even getting our heads around the object of our worship. Praise the God who, being beyond our full understanding or fathoming, benevolently designed us to worship transcendentally. Praise God who, despite the failings of the wisest limited perspective or the most intelligent human perception, made us able to fully function as worshipers of Him.

Praise God!

We cannot know the fullness of God, but we are able to stand in wonder of Him. Worship of God is birthed from wonder. The hair on the back of our neck stands up. We can't look away from the source. Even

---

[58] "Isaiah 29:13-14." The Holy Bible: New International Version. Grand Rapids, MI: Zondervan, 2005. Print.

trying to not worship is to scorn ourselves when we are "astounded with wonder upon wonder".

In Chapter 3, I mentioned an interaction found in the Gospel of John, chapter 4, verse 20. In the story we see Jesus talking to a woman about worship. She wants to talk about the "How" questions. She tells Jesus, "Our fathers worshiped on this mountain, and you people say that in Jerusalem is the place where men ought to worship."[59] Jesus knows that true worship is not about doing the right actions or being at the right place at the right time. He responds to her statement by explaining that "an hour is coming, and now is, when the true worshipers will worship the Father in spirit and truth; for such people the Father seeks to be His worshipers."[60]

The word "spirit" in Jesus' explanation is a translation of the Greek word, πνεῦμα (pneuma), referring to our rational soul, our spiritual discernment, or our very essence as a person. When the truth of God's greatness and goodness collides with the core of who we are, the very part of us that makes us a person, an image bearer of the creator God, the result in us is nothing short of wonder. In turn, that wonder inspires a response of worship.

Spirit + Truth = Wonder.

We've already established that none of us can truly work toward worship. God designed that part of us without an on/off switch. But we can work toward wonder.

---

[59] "John 4:20." New American Standard Bible. La Habra, CA: Foundation Publications, for the Lockman Foundation, 1971. Print.

[60] "John 4:23." New American Standard Bible. La Habra, CA: Foundation Publications, for the Lockman Foundation, 1971. Print.

Working Toward Wonder

So how do we work toward wonder? It's a lot like climbing mountain. Working toward wonder requires orchestrating what we cannot control in concert with what we can control to foster the desired result. In our case the desired result is to worship only God all the time. Let me explain.

Any serious climber should strive to get in great physical shape, procure and become proficient with the best gear possible, and study up on all things concerning the territory, terrain, and timing of summiting the mountain. These activities and exercises all aid the climber in dealing with all the things they cannot control like the mountain, the weather, and any time constraints. In the same way, we have studied up on all the things that we simply cannot control concerning worship. We know that we cannot control that we are hardwired to perceive and rigged to respond. We cannot change the fact that God commands us to worship only Him all the time. We cannot control the three givens that led us to our definition of worship. We cannot control the fact that any attempt to fake a response of worship is outright sinning against God. What we can control is the time we invest in learning about these unchangeable realities and the leg work we put in to understand them. We have already done a lot of work. We only have a little more to do.

The 6 "R"s

I've broken this final few feet of our journey into 3 steps that all start with the same letter, the pirate preference, "R". These steps directly address the disciples dilemma to worship only God all the time despite our limited perspectives and perceptions. In a way, I hope you have a "duh" reaction to all of these. That would mean they make sense, a very important part of a thinking worshiper's world-view.

#1 Research and Remind

#2 Reevaluate and Reassess
#3 Realign and Refocus

#1 Research and Remind

The first step, research and remind, helps us with the "worship God" part of the Disciple's Dilemma to worship only God all the time.

Imagine I put two coins in front of you. Imagine that you had never seen either coin before and that both the coins are printed in a language and with symbols you do not understand. How would you ever know which coin was of greater value? How would you determine each coin's worth? You would have to research what the writing on each coin meant. You would want to find out what the coins were made of and what amount of currency they each represented. It's the same problem we face when we are trying to comprehend the worth of God. Research is necessary if we want to know enough about God to make any sort of assessment of Him. We must actively and thoughtfully collect God data if we are to ever hope to begin to rightly asses His worth. You want to expose your glory receptors to as much stimuli from God as possible. It's hard to assess if God is greater than something else if you know him in only an acquaintance or Facebook kind of way.

Along with any new research, we don't want to forget to compile it with all as much old data we can remember. Using the two coins example again, imagine you knew that in a particular culture a coin's size directly relates to it's worth. If you were able to ascertain the two coins' country of origin, that information plus any new information gained by comparing the sizes of the coins would be very helpful. In the same way, memories of our past interactions with God can shed a great deal of light on comprehending God's worth today. In my second note to worshipers in the first chapter I suggested that you start the spiritual practice of creating "glory albums". I described it as collecting objects and words that remind you of God's past goodness and greatness. It's time to dust those off and spend some time strolling down memory lane. It can be easy to forget ways that God has shown us His greatness and goodness. This is the time to engage those higher functions of our super brains and remember, remember, remember. Any spiritual practice or discipline can aid in this very thing.

#2 Reevaluate and Reassess

The second step, reevaluate and reassess, speaks directly to the "only" part of the Disciple's Dilemma to worship only God all the time.

Now that we have researched and reminded ourselves of God's goodness and greatness, we want to take our newly bolstered perception of God and weigh it against everything else. I mean everything. It's time to reevaluate. This may worry us if were comparing one created thing to all other created things, but God is able to stand up under any and all scrutiny of any measure. We can sometimes be tempted to start down the path of the faker by pretending that those giant things in our lives are no big deal in hopes to lessen the level of competition for God. But God's standing as supreme is not easily shaken. In fact, the trick to preparing ourselves to worship God is not to make little of the big things in our lives to cater to a small God. Instead, we must make so much of God that His greatness and goodness puts everything else in its proper perspective and order of worth.

Imagine a giant scale with God on one side and anything or everything else on the other side. We are reevaluating God by putting him up against anything that competes for our worship of Him. Once we have reevaluated by putting God up against whatever else may be vying for top dog in our world, we reassess. This reassessment will form a new or enhanced perception of God as well as anything on the other side of the scale. If God measures to be of less worth than whatever is on the other side of the scale, that tells us something. It tells us that we either lack a big enough view of God or we have an overinflated view of some other object or focus of worship.

Let's get painfully practical. This is important. When we are faced with a big decision or temptation, here's how this works. Say I am wanting to worship only God all the time, but I am tempted by the control or relief that I perceive I will gain by becoming emotionally or physically involved with another woman besides my wife. I would place that temptation on one side of my imaginary scale and all the data of God's goodness and greatness on the other side. God says to trust in Him and what He says about relationships. The temptation of an affair claims to know better than God and that God is holding out on me. In that moment I have to reassess the competing truth claims.

The trick to coming to an accurate assessment of the results is not to try and diminish the temptation, but to rightly see the hugeness of God's goodness and greatness. This is true for everything we may find ourselves tempted to worship besides God. It's painfully easy to worship the illusion of control; whether it is through manipulating others, by being a know-it-all, or by trying to dictate the events of your life. Minimizing the importance of being in control does not solve the problem. It only treats the symptoms. Though we may try to diminish the real pleasures and pains of finding relief in binging on food or alcohol, tuning out hard relationships, or even by finding release in the arms of someone besides your spouse, it does not lessen the gravity of temptation. The trick is increasing our view of God's great and all-encompassing will. The way out is found by putting the temptation up against the truth of God's good and all-embracing love. When we grasp the power that raised Jesus from the grave, we can let go of fear. When we clearly see God's omnipotence, the mystery of our future is an adventure to be discovered. When we embrace God as Father, any and every expression or manifestation of worship by His children is beautiful no matter how much we personally like or dislike it. When we assess God to be of greatest worth, worship of God will follow.

#3 Realign and Refocus

The third step, realignment and refocusing, helps us with the "all the time" part of the Disciple's Dilemma to worship only God all the time.

We must intentionally realign our life and mind with the life and mind of Christ. In Romans 12:1-2, after gushing in response to the goodness and greatness of God in Romans 11:33-36, Paul gives this exhortation.

"Therefore I urge you, brethren, by the mercies of God, to present your bodies a living and holy sacrifice, acceptable to God, which is your spiritual service of worship. And do not be conformed to this world, but be transformed by the renewing of your mind, so that you may prove what the will of God is, that which is good and acceptable and perfect."[61]

The word "spiritual" in this passage is translated from the Greek word λογικὴν (logikēn) and refers to our reasonable or rational faculties. Paul is making the argument that the most rational thing to do in light of our researching and reminding, our reevaluating and reassessing, is to realign all of who we are-body, soul, and mind-with the truth of who God is. This is what theologians refer to as sanctification. It is a part of us working toward wonder to birth a response of worship. It makes perfect sense to believe in the impossible when we have aligned our understanding with

[61] "Romans 12:1-2." New American Standard Bible. La Habra, CA: Foundation Publications, for the Lockman Foundation, 1971. Print.

the reality of who God is and what he has done. It is completely rational to trust the unfathomable when we see everything from God's perspective. We realign ourselves with Christ by doing what he did; making sure we perceive as much of God's glory as possible and creating the space so that a worship response flows naturally. My favorite argument in favor of daily engagement with the Bible is that it allows us to realign our perspective to match God's perspective. It is so much more than simply reviewing the same passages over and over and over again. It is realigning our ever changing lives with the never changing word of God. God's perspective is the true perspective, and, by extension, the truth.

As we realign our perceptions with God's perspective of reality (the only true reality) our eyes will start to refocus to see how God sees the world. Things that seemed to be important and were always crystal-clear from your idol or self-worshiping perspective will become less important and less in-focus as we start to look from God's perspective. Things that are important to God will become more in focus and more important to us. We won't be able to see with the same scope, but our focus will start to follow His. When we refocus on the things that God keeps in focus, the things important and in alignment with His perfect will, they become important to us as well.

The wonderful thing is, these three steps are a self-feeding loop. As we realign our perspective with God's perspective, our focus is tuned to capture as much of God's glory as possible. This in turn greatly affects our perceptions, which then dictate our response of worship. This then feeds the research part of our work toward wonder, and the cycle starts again. That's how we work toward wonder and how someone can authentically and honestly strive to worship only God all the time.

A Case Study

Let's see how this plays out by using a popular figure in the Bible as a case study for working toward wonder. King David in the Old Testament was a fugitive, led rebel armies, and killed a lot of people. He was also apparently pretty good with a harp and an accomplished songwriter. Not a lot of modern day equivalents pop into mind as we take a look at his life, but his songs, especially those recorded in the book of Psalms, ring with a certain truth, an approachability that welcomes all of us. I think this is because David understood what we have talked about in this book. I'm sure he would have much more to add to the conversation if he were physically present and, believe me, I would much rather read his book on worship than write my own. But we do have some of his songs. As a songwriter myself, I tell people that I pretty much write the soundtrack to my own life. That was true of David. So let's take a look at how David responded to God and see if we can follow his path to work toward wonder. Let's use Psalm 103 as a case study.

Psalm 103

1 Praise the LORD, O my soul; all my inmost being, praise his holy name.

David starts by commanding his soul to worship. He is being proactive, not just passive. He knows that in light of all the things that compete for the position of greatest worth in his perception of the world, it is an act of faith to take the initiative to work toward wonder and worship only God all the time. David could have gone the way of the faker and said,

"My soul *is* praising the Lord. All my inmost being *is* praising His holy name.", but he didn't. He honestly acknowledged that he was volitionally having to choose to work toward wonder at that time in his life. David quickly continues to spend a good amount of time to research and remind himself of the goodness and greatness of God.

2 Praise the LORD, O my soul,

and forget not all his benefits-

3 who forgives all your sins

and heals all your diseases,

4 who redeems your life from the pit

and crowns you with love and compassion,

5 who satisfies your desires with good things

so that your youth is renewed like the eagle's.

6 The LORD works righteousness

and justice for all the oppressed.

7 He made known his ways to Moses,

his deeds to the people of Israel:

8 The LORD is compassionate and gracious,

slow to anger, abounding in love.

9 He will not always accuse,

nor will he harbor his anger forever;

10 He does not treat us as our sins deserve

or repay us according to our iniquities.

11 For as high as the heavens are above the earth,

so great is his love for those who fear him;

12 as far as the east is from the west,

so far has he removed our transgressions from us.

13 As a father has compassion on his children,

so the LORD has compassion on those who fear him;

David makes a long list, poring over memories of God's goodness and greatness, to research and remind himself of who exactly is competing against any and everything else in his life for position of greatest worth. David then cuts to the chase to reevaluate and reassess God's worth in comparison to His biggest rival for worship. Let's see how man measures up against God.

14 for he (God) knows how we are formed,

    he remembers that we are dust.

15 As for man, his days are like grass,

    he flourishes like a flower of the field;

16 the wind blows over it and it is gone,

    and its place remembers it no more.

17 But from everlasting to everlasting

    the LORD's love is with those who fear him,

    and his righteousness with their children's children-

18 with those who keep his covenant

    and remember to obey his precepts.

19 The LORD has established his throne in heaven,

    and his kingdom rules over all.

God is the creator. God is not just an innovator, He started from scratch. We are not canned or assembly-line-constructed. He is the starter and finisher of all creation including us. Man is the created. Man may have a temporary lifetime of fame, but will eventually die and be forgotten. Conversely, God is everlasting. His goodness and greatness, brazenly expressed in love, lasts forever. His fame and His power will never fade. Ultimately, David correctly concludes that God wins and holds the title of greatest worth even in comparison to himself, or any other member of the human race for that matter.

David ends Psalm 103 by realigning his perceptions of the world with the truth of who God is and a call to others to do the same. David is all about God's glory and desires that all His creation, including people, would have a natural response of worship to only God all the time.

20 Praise the LORD, you his angels,

    you mighty ones who do his bidding,

who obey his word.

21 Praise the LORD, all his heavenly hosts,

you his servants who do his will.

22 Praise the LORD, all his works

everywhere in his dominion.

Praise the LORD, O my soul.

So there you have it, even King David worked toward wonder. In the face of circumstances that I could never imagine, David still worshiped God in spirit and truth. There was no faking in this case. Just like David, we too can find ourselves in crazy circumstances, but our hope to worship God does not depend on our circumstances, it depends on our ability to work toward wonder, to let ourselves be consumed by the flood of God's goodness and greatness.

In Conclusion

High performance, state of the art worship engines come standard in every model of human being. That by no means implies it is ordinary. We have spent the duration of this book marveling at the wonders of God's design for us to function as full-on worshipers of only Him all the time. Looking back, I hope this chapter about the "hows" of working toward wonder gives a kind of 20/20 hindsight to the necessity of all the previous chapters. When we grab onto the first definition we come across or quickly acquired conclusions, we can often times find ourselves with a bunch of answers to the wrong questions. I'm glad you've come on this journey with me to thoroughly ask the all-important "whys" to support and give context to this short chapter of "hows".

There is one more huge similarity between summiting a mountain peak and working toward wonder. Most people spend very little time at the top of any mountain. They know that it was never about quantity. For the money, time, and energy invested, they could have plastered posters of other mountaineer's pictures of the view from the top to every surface of their homes many times over. No, just like climbing, worship is about quality. We can't leech off of another's experiences or live in a single great moment in the past. We have to see God's goodness and greatness right now with our own eyes. Praise God that we can work toward it. He has designed us with everything we need to work towards wonder and ultimately respond to Him in worship.

A Note To Worshipers #7
concerning lament

Hello friend,

Over the years, one topic has seemed almost paradoxical in its nature as an expression of an authentic worship response. That topic is the sticky issue of lament. How is it that we see huge portions of scripture, including an entire book titled Lamentations, devoted to the struggles of those working toward wonder?

The key lies in the difference between complaining and lamenting. Complaining is just stating how bad things are. Lament is our response to having seen and experienced for ourselves God's goodness and greatness, but the current perception of our circumstances don't add up with our God albums. We can fake our way through tragedy by repeating mantras and slogans until we are blue in the face, but we will never come to a place of authentic worship. However, if we cry out to God because of, not in spite of, how this tragedy shakes our perception of His goodness and greatness, that is Biblical lament. An authentic response of worship takes the form of lament when we are asking, "God, how could this unthinkable thing happen when I know you to be so good and great?". That's why in the psalms you see a lot of the following order:

1. God, this situation or tragedy seems to be in direct competition with your goodness and greatness.

2. So, I will acknowledge what's broken while intentionally working toward wonder.

Some of the greatest moments in my own God albums are memories of God again and again showing His goodness and greatness through and despite tragedy. This is the stuff ebenezers are made of. My prayer is that you *will allow God to show Himself to be good and great despite the seemingly overwhelming size of whatever tragedy may be competing for your worship. We don't want to fake it in a vain attempt to "protect" God from having to be reevaluated and reassessed. Lament isn't a denial of God. Lament is wrestling with tragedy, pain, and sometimes death because of and in context of all that God is and does.*

God bless and keep you,

Jeremy

Letter To Worship Leaders - vii
concerning evaluation

Dear Wonder Watcher,

In my first letter I talked to you about Mount Everest. Summiting Mount Everest is a journey that starts way before one arrives at Base Camp. You don't just wake up one day and say to yourself, "I think I'll climb Everest today." There is a lot of preparation involved. It can take months. But with a lot of training, time, and money there can come a day when you actually do wake up absolutely planning to summit the tallest mountain on the planet. Except it won't be in a singsong voice over coffee, because you will be starting around 11:00pm the night before in the Death Zone (8,000 ft plus) and gasping for oxygen as you cough out the words, "Let's do this, take some pictures, and get the heck off this deathtrap."[62] Thankfully, our conversation concerning worship hasn't required such a monumental effort.[63]

However, we all have been in meetings that sometimes felt like they were sucking the very life out of us. I want to talk about something that may be the worst part of your week; the evaluation of your last attempt to facilitate worship with and for a group of other people all on their own journey and with their own perspectives, perceptions, and subsequent responses. Please listen closely to what I am about to say next.

You can't make or stop anyone from worshiping.

---

[62] "The Route - Climbers Guide to Everest." The Route - Climbers Guide to Everest. Web. 04 Nov. 2013.

[63] I hope. Is someone making you read this? Sorry. I never meant this conversation to be forced. Not that you'll ever know that, because when I or anyone is given compulsory reading the endnotes are the first to be skipped.

Not only do you not have ability to make anyone worship, you do not have the responsibility to make anyone worship.

All the perfect songs can be sung, the pyrotechnics can go off without a hitch, and you can outperform Freddie Mercury, but if those you are leading don't perceive God to be of greatest worth, they WILL NOT worship Him.[64] On the contrary, If people are captivated by the goodness and greatness of their creator, you could get up there, drool all over yourself, and do your best wiggle dance, and the people would worship God for unconditionally loving and giving life to their "challenged" worship leader.

So, how or what do we evaluate? Do we continue to grade our events by number of attenders or breathe a sigh of relief when "God shows up" as if he wasn't there already?

Again, I invoke Paul, "By no means!"

Jesus explained worship as being all about spirit and truth. It is vital that you are engaging in your own spiritual practices or disciplines and that you have a real, working, and loving relationship with God. This is so that you may personally testify and point people to all He is and all He has done in others' lives and mostly your own. More than anything else, engaging in spiritual practices that help you become more like Christ and grow closer to God is the very first task of any worship leader. It's more important than song selection, order of service, or even to can or not to can the junior high bake sale skit. Directly after this task is the task of encouraging and discipling those you lead to do the same; find and engage in spiritual practices that widen their view of God and

---

[64] "Freddie Mercury Biography." Bio.com. A&E Networks Television. Web. 04 Nov. 2013.

help them become more like Jesus. You are not in the pep rally or motivational game. You are in the spiritual formation and transformation game.

What I'm not saying: Don't work hard because it doesn't matter.

What I am saying: Let your evaluations focus primarily on you and the people you lead perceiving God as being of greatest worth.

Work your tail off to be good tour guides and facilitators, but never let someone else's response be the measure for your labors. It is between you and God and a few trusted friends walking with you if you gave your absolute best or not. God designed all of us so that the rest takes care of itself.

I hope this frees you. Actually, you are free. I hope you recognize it. I hope those you work with/for recognize it. Thank you for your time.

Blessings to you and your work,

Jeremy Pape

Chapter 6 Discussion Questions

Describe a time you were filled with wonder or awe.

How do you feel about the idea of working toward a natural response?

What is the one thing you want to take with you from what has been discussed in this book?

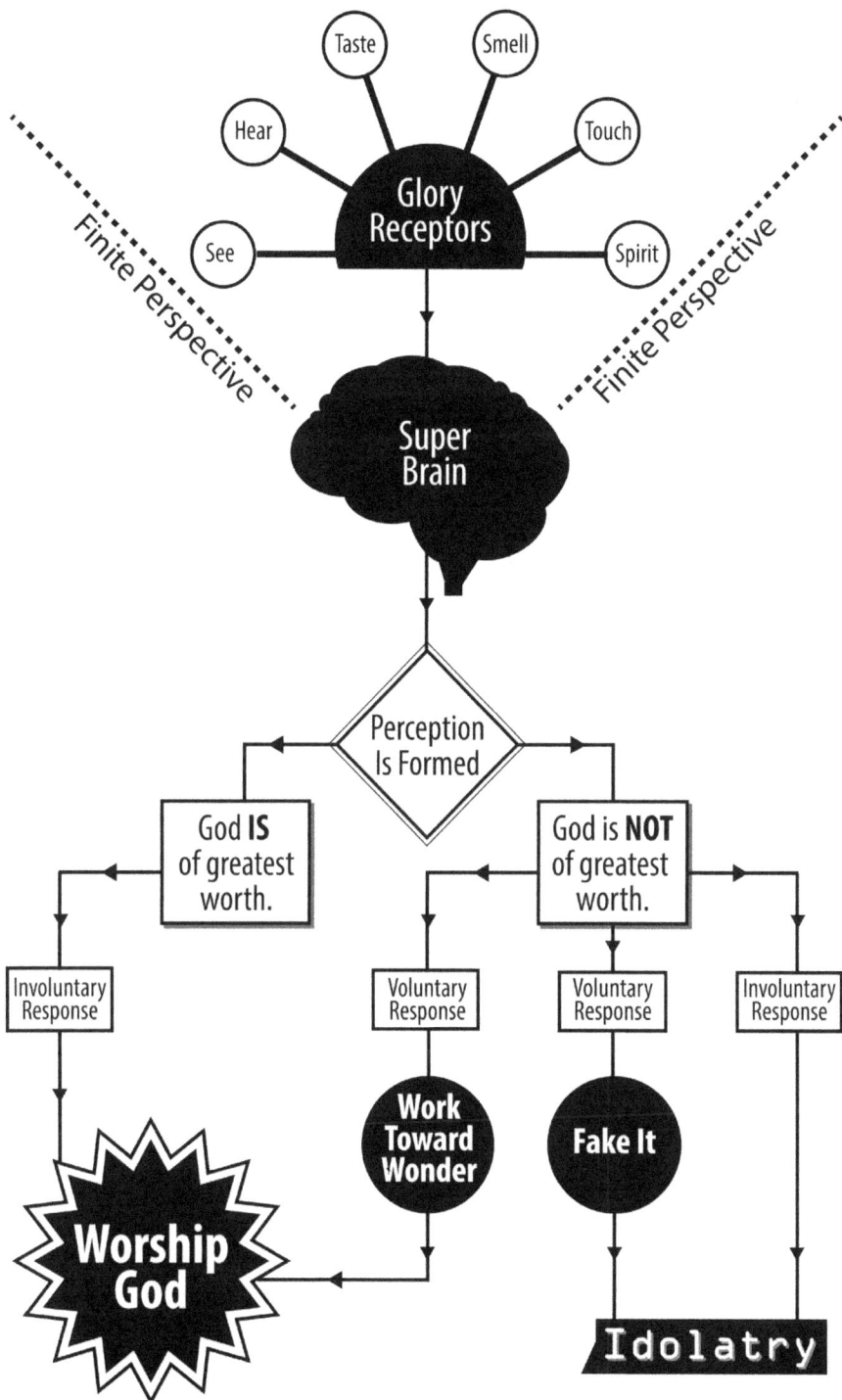

Taste

Smell

Hear

Touch

Glory Receptors

See

Spirit

Finite Perspective

Finite Perspective

Super Brain

Perception Is Formed

God **IS** of greatest worth.

God is **NOT** of greatest worth.

Involuntary Response

Voluntary Response

Voluntary Response

Involuntary Response

Work Toward Wonder

Fake It

Worship God

Idolatry

FINAL THOUGHTS

So where do we go from here? We've taken our backstage tour to reveal what worship is and how to pursue it. How do we apply all this to become mature worshipers of God? How can we help others work toward wonder?

First we start with what we know.

- We know that we are hardwired to perceive. There is no on or off switch.
- We are rigged to respond. We always respond to perceptions formed with our super brains.
- Worship is the natural human response to anything of greatest worth.
- As followers of Christ, we are faced with the Disciple's Dilemma; to worship only God all the time.
- We know that no matter how pure or good our intentions, God hates it when we fake it.

- We know that working toward wonder may take intentional implementation of proven means, but in the end is the only way to authentically find a solution to the Disciple's Dilemma.

We know quite a bit. Now that we have a theologically and logically sound Biblical understanding of worship, we can enter into the larger, universal worship conversation that has spanned Church history in a way that is both respectful and helpful. Here are a few ideas or challenges to chew on and explore. Where you go next is up to you.

First, King David was called a man after God's own heart. Was David's dealing with the command to worship only God all the time a one and done issue for him? Absolutely not. The air time the Bible gives David's story including a huge chunk of the psalms is testimony to how God responded when David both worked toward wonder and when he ended up faking it. Like David, we all have and will blow it. We will always struggle to worship only God all the time. But like David, we will also sometimes be gloriously successful.

Does this make the contents of this book just some pie in the sky idealism?

No. In fact, any good Christian methodology including working towards wonder will highlight our need for the grace found through faith in Jesus Christ instead of building up our own self-dependence. The disciple's dilemma is not mastered in this life. We have to daily throw ourselves at the cross of Christ. Believe you me, this is a much better place than at the cross of public opinion or passing fads. We are all in process to know and become more and more like Christ. The good news of the Gospel is that we can pursue worshiping only God all the time in the context of His grace and the complete and completed work of Christ. The way God designed us to be worshipers screams that the pursuit of worshiping

Him is a pursuit for those seeking maturity, not for those casually placated by the occasional happy accident or a lucky experience.

Second, the contents of this book will also help us better interact with the macro, intergenerational worship conversation. Taking some baby steps concerning how we talk about worship, evaluate worship, or even what we label as "worship" will serve all of us in leaps and bounds. Understanding worship to first be a response and not an adjective will greatly clarify things. Knowing that why we worship is more important than how we worship will make strategies and facilitation of community and private responses to God much more fruitful. A clear and defined starting line of "why" questions will create a kind of on-ramp for everyone to enter and be relevant to the worship conversation for years to come.

Last, I hope that what we know about worship will give us an urgency to lovingly walk alongside and offer grace and help to those we come across that are lost in their own fakery. So many followers of Christ are still operating with the mindset of "fake it till you make it". This is sadly not because of a conscious choice between authenticity and hypocrisy, but because they simply know of no other way. How could we leave them to their fate? A well-timed comment or suggestion to work toward wonder could make all the difference. You and I could be a first wave of sympathetic brothers and sisters inviting them out of insanity and into a holistic obedience to God's command to worship only Him all the time.

In the end, both followers of Christ as well as those that are not yet convinced are designed to live lives fully responding to the goodness and greatness of God whether they do or do not. My prayer for you and all of us is that the contents of this book will aid and inspire us to see more and more of both God's goodness and His greatness with greater frequency. When that happens, an increase in worship of God is inevitable. I also pray that we would see a real and productive change sweep over the worship landscape, first in our own hearts, and then among the world-wide community of believers.

Thank you for joining me for this leg of our worship journey. My parting words for you, friend, are these.

Look to be surprised by His goodness.

Search until you are in awe of His greatness.

Take the advice given to Job to "stand and consider the wonders of God."[65]

---

[65] "Job 37:14." New American Standard Bible. La Habra, CA: Foundation Publications, for the Lockman Foundation, 1971. Print.

ACKNOWLEDGMENTS

I want to thank the students, leaders, and alumni of Christian Challenge at the University of Nebraska at Lincoln. They have always pushed me to be as thorough and clear as possible when it comes to my beliefs. I never would have come to write this book if not for their insistence that I explore and scrutinize my own inner worship engine. I also want to thank Brett for allowing me the freedom to start writing this book and I want to thank Tyler for always asking when I would finally finish it.

I would not have been able to write this without the years invested in me by great worship leaders like Lentz and Robbie. I also am hugely grateful to Patrick, Liam, Tim, and Dee Anne who have offered invaluable comments and critique in shaping this book. I must especially thank Allison for her mad proofreading skills because anyone who knows me knows I couldn't spell my way out of a wet paper bag.

I also want to send a shout out to my dad for showing me how to string 3 points together in an orderly way week after week, sermon after sermon. Thanks to my mom for always valuing education and working to pay for mine. And especially thank you to my wife, Amber, for being my biggest cheerleader and fan.

ABOUT THE AUTHOR

Jeremy Pape was born in Nebraska and raised in Kansas. He studied at Kansas State University and Emmanuel House Seminary. He has worked to share the Gospel of the Kingdom of God in higher education for the past 11 years both in the United States and abroad. He currently lives in Lincoln, Nebraska with his wife and two young sons.

www.ingramcontent.com/pod-product-compliance
Lightning Source LLC
Chambersburg PA
CBHW060507030426
42337CB00015B/1776